HOLLYWOOD
SAMIZDAT

HOLLYWOOD SAMIZDAT

NOTES FROM BELOW THE LINE

RAMBO VAN HALEN

PASSAGE
PUBLISHING

For information, contact support@passage.press.

Trade paperback ISBN: 978-1-959403-60-9

Cover design by Wide Dog

Library of Congress Control Number: 2025937273

Passage Publishing
Los Angeles, CA
www.passage.press

Printed in the United States of America

1 3 5 7 9 10 8 6 4 2

Passage Publishing
www.passage.press

Dedicated to all the oracles.

And to Anita, who told me not to be afraid.

CONTENTS

SUSHI DINNER

I was eating dinner by myself at a sushi bar in Venice. I had moved out of LA at this point, but I still flew back for work every other week or so. There was a bad date happening next to me. Girl was smoking hot—like model hot. Dude was a giant nerd. He was talking about the superiority of *Star Trek* over *Star Wars*. Then gamer talk. Then something about software development. Girl was bored shitless.

But whatever. I was minding my own business, drinking beer and eating sashimi.

I chatted with the chef and bought his guys a round. He asked me if I lived in the neighborhood. I said I used to, but that I moved out of state and was back for work for a few days. Then new sushi-chef friend asked me the dreaded "So what do you do?" question. And I said the magic word: *producer* . . .

When I'm in public, with people I don't know, I usually lie about what I do. Once I was cornered in a Starbucks in the Ralphs on Lincoln near LAX by an old queen who pegged me as a producer. It must have been my stressed-out look and the producer uniform of jeans and a black T-shirt. After a while, those in the know can tell who's who.

He opened with, "Excuse me, are you a producer?" I admitted that I was and then he tried to pitch me his script. He went from flirty to angry as I kept trying to explain I wasn't *that* type of producer. By the end he was screaming, "CAN I SEND IT TO YOU? PLEASE? IT'S *REALLY* GOOD!"

I had to shove him out of the way. Left without my coffee.

After that I started lying. "Project manager," I'd say. Sometimes I'd make up something ridiculous, like underwater welder or that I was a cheese merchant.

That fucking question. Every party, every flight, every just sitting on a bench looking at the ocean, that fucking question: "So what do you do?"

If I happen to chat with someone who stays away from The Question, then I know they're in The Business. This happened on a long ski-lift ride. We were sitting on the lift chatting. I learned he was from LA but he skipped The Question. That piqued my interest (because everyone asks The Question), so I asked if he did industry stuff.

Turned out he was a big director. You've seen his movies. Great guy.

We had a good chat about everything but The Business. Just normal dad-to-dad conversation. Didn't offer my card because I know what that's like. He was just trying to ski and have fun.

He skied off and I'll never see him again.

But that night in Venice I had a few beers in me and the sushi was good. I fucked up. I answered The Question and said the magic words: "I'm a producer."

Instantly, I felt a change in bad date girl. She froze when I said the word. There was a pause followed by heat. I could feel the pause and I could feel her heat.

Then she cut her date off mid-sentence. She pivoted on her seat, told me my sashimi looked "yummy." Asked to try it. I obliged and she slurped it up in that faux-clumsy seductively flirtatious way only a hot chick can pull off.

And now she had turned her entire attention to me. Started touching me and giggling. Even touched my cock at one point. She was coming on like a stripper. She was hot but her approach was too strong. It was a turnoff. So I mentioned something about my wife and (at the time, young) kids, to get her back on task with her date.

It didn't work.

More than being turned off by the Stripper Flirt, I was embarrassed to be party to poor Nerdy Date's humiliation. He seemed like a nice guy. Intelligent, kind. He didn't deserve this.

So I cut it short, got my check, and left.

As I was waiting for my Uber, she came outside. The ocean air was cold, and she was wearing something sheer and low cut, no bra, nipples popping. Kept chatting. Flirty body language, suggestive eyes. She was starting to shiver but kept going.

Uber showed so I jumped in and went.

Bye bitch.

▩▩▩▩▩

I was (and am) a nobody in Hollywood. I'm more of a nobody now than I ever was. But for a time I held the title "producer." It's an amorphous title. There are lots of types of producers. I was a "line producer," which is part project manager, part accountant. This is mid-level management, but it took a long time and a lot of hard work for me to get there.

I started at the bottom as a production assistant (PA). That's the most junior member of any crew. The guy who gets coffee and runs errands or works under the assistant directors to help run the set. But I worked my way up. And just like this book isn't a linear story, I moved up in a non-linear fashion with lots of little detours along the way.

The short story, ignoring the detours, is that after working as a PA I became a production coordinator. After that, I worked as a production manager and eventually a line producer. As of this writing I haven't produced anything in more than five years. I've left LA but I still work in the industry. These days I consult and do specialized union crew work in a small market.

Oh—and I have more fun now than I did as a producer. That's for damn sure.

As a line producer, I had a certain amount of power and enjoyed certain perks. I had a staff of PAs and other assistants who would drive me from airports to meetings and fetch me lunch and booze and take and make calls as directed. I had the discretion to hire and fire and spend large sums of money. I sat in on meetings with major players, sometimes had input on who to cast, and generally helped bring productions from concept to completion.

That said, I wasn't a Harvey Weinstein or a Scott Rudin. I didn't have the power to green light a project or fire a director or hire an Oscar winner. I never made anyone rich or famous.

However, that didn't stop women (and sometimes men) from coming on to me.

This type of thing happened quite often, in fact. It puzzled me for many years.

I was a decent-looking guy, reasonably fit, of average height, and made okay money. And so, while I never saw myself as a supremely attractive man, to the wannabe actress waiting tables, I was a big catch.

On the inside (from my perspective) there's no glamor in The Business, but someone trying to break in would meet me and picture themselves on the red carpet.

At the time, I was completely oblivious to this, but eventually I came to figure it out. They thought I had the power to change their life. But I didn't. I wasn't that guy.

■■■■■

For most of Western history, going back at least to the ancient Greeks, performers were seen as the equivalent of prostitutes. The acting/singing/dancing was just an ad for the real goods. Nineteenth-century opera divas were especially famous for this. Some even had boudoirs built backstage.

Strippers are maybe the best contemporary analogy. Climbing the pole is just a way to get a john into the champagne room.

Until the early twentieth century, any kind of public entertainment was mainly a front for prostitution. The old Vaudeville joke is that "Vaudevillian" really means "opened for the stripper."

But with the invention of Hollywood, acting became respectable. I believe this has to do with the medium of film. You "watch" a play, but you "look" into a movie. It's reflexive. Humans are programed to track motion, which activates dedicated neural pathways. As such we pay attention when we see a moving object. But the moving objects on the screen aren't real. They're just reflected light. But even though we know the images are not real, they *feel* real. The resulting cognitive dissonance results in the movie hacking your brain, suspending your disbelief, and leaving you changed. It's like a form of hypnosis.

Don't believe me? The next time you're at the movies, sit in the front row and periodically turn around to look at the audience. They're transfixed. They're hypnotized.

And unlike a play, you can't just walk backstage with a dozen roses and a pocketful of cash and expect to get it on with the lead actress.

You don't see the performers on the street. They don't live in your neighborhood. Your mother doesn't know their mother. They live in a sunny place at the edge of the continent but somehow magically travel to your little shit town to entertain you. These aren't people. They're living gods.

But what is this thing we call acting? The proverbial Martian (first time on Earth, reporting on the humans, preparing invasion plans) might conclude that these actors who pretend to be other people are mentally ill. And in many cases, I've found this to be true.

Most actors are nice, normal-ish people with quirks, but the "method" actors . . . watch out. Most of them would be in prison if they weren't famous. The only time they're sane is when they're acting.

▪▪▪▪

Murder scenes can be really disturbing. Not "action" scenes where it's good guys shooting it out with bad guys or a car chase that ends in a fiery crash. Those types of scenes are hyper-stylized. They're almost cartoonish when you see them in person.

What I'm talking about here is murder. Homicide. Where we simulate the intentional taking of human life. The disturbing part isn't the fake blood, or the exploding squibs, or the firing of the gun. It's the malevolent energy. The energy of murderous rage.

The first murder scene I did was with a famous Method Guy. He was a tough guy. Dangerous in real life. And after the rehearsal, when we were rolling camera, he wasn't acting. He truly went *there*. The rage he filled himself with was so palpable and so terrifying that I have never forgotten it. This wasn't playacting. In a very literal sense, he physically and emotionally "performed" the most vile and base act that a human being can do.

The scene was set in a waiting room. The camera rolled, and Method Guy momentarily just sat there, nervous but quiet. This was the part of the movie where his character transformed from a merely troubled man into a vicious monster. It started with slow breathing, which slowly became quicker. Then his eyes started darting around the set. His eyes were moving faster and faster. Suddenly Method Guy snapped. He sprang out of his seat with crazed furious eyes, ran to the victim, shot him in the head, and sprinted off. There was little blood, but the energy—it was horrifying.

We had a number of extras on set. They had been told by the assistant directors to stay quiet but pantomime shock and fear. But their fear was real. Some of them screamed. My jaw fell open. I was frozen with shock.

The veteran stunt guy he "killed" was pretty shaken up too. There was a second take, but stunt guy was now freaked and anticipated the murder. I was freaked as well. I had nightmares for weeks.

This is why he was a famous actor. Because he could go to the darkest places, the places normal people don't want to visit. And perhaps even more disturbingly, not only did he go there, he *thrived* there. He was *comfortable* there. He was in a familiar place—it was like he was home.

Aside from a mild form of mental illness, another quality required to be successful in acting is compliance, more commonly referred to as being able to "take direction."

By the time an actress gets to a callback session in front of a director, it's already been established that she has the right look, age, body type, etc. The only question the director needs answered is, "Can I direct you?" or, "Do you understand what I want, and will you do as I say?"

Because otherwise what's the point, right?

Someone who can't take direction is known as having "limited range." Woody Allen is a great example of this. Allan Konigsberg plays the same character in every movie he's ever made. And no, he's not playing himself. He's playing the only character he knows how to play, which the world knows as Woody Allen. (But then again, he's usually directing himself, so it all works out.)

Acting is a competitive game, so a large degree of ambition is required in order to make it. Every year thousands of the most beautiful people in the world move to LA (land of the gods) to be famous (and become gods themselves).

Of those, only one or two will actually ever make it. Hollywood is not a meritocracy, and the ones who end up on top have to leverage their assets. For an actress, their chief assets are their beauty and their sexuality. So it's no surprise they use their assets to get what they want.

▪▪▪▪▪

I was doing a callback casting session for a national-broadcast beer commercial. We were looking for an actress in a bikini. We were seeing about eighty women that day.

Bikini-clad woman after bikini-clad woman comes into the room, flirts with us, says the line, then leaves. Sometime after lunch, like hour seven of bikini casting, a fully clothed actress walked in.

She explained, in a cute hot-mess ditzy way, that she was running late, had forgot her bikini, but would we mind if she auditioned in her underwear?

Being polite gentlemen, we obliged, and in an effortlessly seductive way she stripped down to her see-through Agent Provocateurs. She said the line, took some direction (compliance!), said the line again, got dressed (effortlessly seductive), and left.

I was rock hard. We all were.

Needless to say, she got the part. I've never had commercial talent approved that quickly. I nodded, the director made a thumbs up, the agency guys nodded, and the client said, "Book her." It took less than five seconds. She hadn't even left the building.

Of course she played us. There was no way she was wearing that lingerie on a random weekday afternoon in the Valley. And there was no way a professional actress would forget her bikini for a big casting session that specifically called for her to wear a bikini. I think she was a friend of the casting director, and he probably suggested the stunt seeing how bored we were (and it was probably not the only time he pulled this).

And of course, we knew we had been played. But we loved every second of it and (this is important) she did too.

Agent Provocateur leveraged her assets and beat out eighty other women. She probably made $100k for that one-day shoot. It beats waiting tables.

But it does beg the question: would she have leveraged *all* of her assets and fucked me for the part? I'm not sure. She was a nice girl, so I'd hate to think that. And in the end she didn't need to fuck anybody for the part—she got it without going there.

(And no, the casting director wasn't banging her. He was gay.)

But what if it was a big role? A life-changing role that would make her a living god to the people back home? I think she and every other actress in the world would go there.

Not every woman, but definitely every actress.

Ambitious, compliant, and a little crazy. Then add in the fact she also wants to be a living god. *That's* an actress.

How many ambitious, compliant, slightly mentally ill women went to Harvey Weinstein's hotel suite to perform the "forgot my bikini" stunt? Or the "my boyfriend is getting abusive and I'm afraid to go home tonight" stunt?

The best way to pull this off is to make a man think it was all *his* idea. His skills of seduction. His power. His status. His generosity of letting her audition without a bikini.

All women know this. But actresses know this especially well.

Now, this is not just analogous to prostitution—it *is* prostitution. And like all prostitutes, actresses feel guilt. And the more pleasurable it is, the more guilt they feel.

Adding to the guilt is the anxiety of knowing that the clock is running out. Their assets (beauty, sexuality, etc.) are perishable. Maybe they get a decade. Maybe less. Time comes for all of us. Women are acutely aware of this fact.

Victim worship was only part of the "Me Too" story. By assuming the mantle of victim and martyr these women were absolved of the stigma of whoredom and the public shaming that came with it. It was a secular general absolution.

Men like Terry Richardson and Harvey Weinstein walked that line—and may have crossed it. But most of the allegations were bullshit, made by women who knew exactly what they were after and knew exactly how to get it (and in most cases *did* get it).

Much was lost with Me Too. One of the ironies is that sexy actresses are no longer in vogue. And this is a tragedy. Women like Agent Provocateur worked hard for what they had.

Effortless beauty isn't effortless. And now an entire generation of sexy would-be demigods is aging out before they can reach Olympus.

But some things never change. Women certainly haven't changed. A woman almost bailed in the middle of a sushi date for the chance to be with a mid-level paper-pushing producer.

What would she do for a real shot at fame and fortune?

What would any of us do to become a god?

WAR STORIES

The business of Hollywood is storytelling. That's the core of what we do.

It's an amazing thing when you think about it. An entire industry with hundreds of thousands of workers based solely on the power of storytelling—something people used to just sit around and do for free.

At its peak in 2019, box office totals for the United States and Canada were more than $11 billion dollars. And that doesn't include television advertising revenue, streaming service subscriptions, and all other types of visual media.

This is big business. It's certainly real money to me.

And even though I was (and still am) a cog in this giant machine called the Entertainment Industry—an industry based on the power of story—the thing I have the most trouble with is telling my story to myself.

━━━━━

Many film workers—that is, the people who create movies, TV shows, and commercials—are afflicted by addiction and alcoholism. You can include me in that cohort. I've come to believe it's an occupational hazard. The reasons why aren't important for now (we'll get to that later), but the solution is.

Every alcoholic and addict gets to a point where he can no longer continue. So how could I? Once the drinking started, it became compulsive, and I would not stop until I was so drunk that I was physically incapable of getting the glass to my mouth.

Of course everyone around you knows your secret. They know even before you do. You're always the *last* one to know. That's just how addiction works.

But when you finally realize you have a problem, and you're free-falling at terminal velocity barreling straight for the ground, you run into a paradox: you realize you can't go on living your life under the influence, but you can't imagine a life of sobriety.

At this point you either find a way to get sober, or you end your life. Many do end their lives—usually by unintentional overdose or drinking themselves to death.

But fortunately for me I chose the other path and got sober. As of this writing I haven't had a drink in more than ten years.

I did it with the help of Alcoholics Anonymous (AA). This is the seminal twelve step program. The point of the twelve steps is to allow you to lead your life in such a way that you don't need to get drunk or get high. It's a way to "deal with life on life's terms," as they say in AA.

Because life is hard.

And this world can be a shitty place.

Maybe you were raised by a neurotic actress. Or your father (that you never really knew) died when you were young. And then you came down with a crippling illness at what should have been the prime of your life. And then you ended up in a so-called glamorous line of work where you're easily replaceable and people would do anything and everything short of murder to get ahead of you and everybody else. And you have to go to work every day and deal with these people. And they're disagreeable and dishonest and abusive and sometimes straight-up insane. But you still have to deal. You can't walk away, because you love it. Or at least, you tell yourself that you love it, in part because you don't have anything better to walk away to. . . .

So you're stuck. And wouldn't a drink help right about now? Wouldn't it make you feel better? Wouldn't it help you deal with the stress and the anger and the resentment? Everyone needs a time-out once in a while. Everyone needs a little break.

Actually, I *do* think I deserve a little break. I *do* think I deserve to feel good—right?

(Right?)

So I take a drink. Suddenly I'm drunk again. And I can't stop. Then I'm right back where I started. It's a nightmarish cycle, and it leads only one way.

But thanks to a twelve-step program, I killed the cycle before it killed me. Aside from finding a higher power, the most important part of it for me was this: the need to be honest. The need to be honest with myself and with everyone in my life.

In the program they call it "rigorous" honesty.

The thing I struggle with is telling my story to myself. Because sometimes I don't know the truth of what happened. Part of that is because of time, but another part of it is because of the booze and the pills. Some things are hazy and some things are just missing.

And no, this isn't a book about addiction and recovery. It's a book about me. It's a book about me telling my story to myself.

[•••••]

In fact, there are many stories that I want to tell. Though it's not a "want" as much as a "need." The Business is such a weird fucking place. Anyone who doesn't have firsthand experience of it can't really comprehend what goes on there. It's too strange. Too foreign. Too out of the bounds of normal life.

Maybe it's an experience akin to war. War is so outside the bounds of normal human experience that most people have no clue what it really entails. Only veterans can discuss it with each other in a truly meaningful way.

Ever overhear two vets talk about their deployments? I understand the words, but I don't get the meaning. Then again, I've never been to war.

I had a Marine buddy. He started working for me as my assistant, but we became friends. This was Iraq War. Peak Global War on Terror.

My assistants kept burning out due to the stress of the job, so I started recruiting combat vets thinking they'd be able to handle it. A film set is nothing like combat, right? It turned out they burned out faster than the run-of-the-mill PA.

So my Marine buddy was at Fallujah. He had demons. He needed to tell his stories.

We'd be driving and he'd just gush. But the stories didn't make any sense. It was just random disjointed vignettes of fucked-up bizarre shit. And there was no moral or meaning to any of it.

I didn't understand this until I read Tim O'Brien's *The Things They Carried*. He was telling TRUE war stories, not the fake ones that have a moral and make sense. My Marine's stories made no sense, but they were true. And they were true because they made no sense.

You can see this in the 1980 film *The Big Red One*, starring Mark Hamill and Lee Marvin. Veterans, including my grandfather who served in the Second World War, have told me it's the most realistic war movie ever made. It's based on director Samuel Fuller's experiences in the war. But it made no sense to me. It's just a collection of bizarre vignettes.

My Marine buddy needed to talk. And talk he did. About how the feral dogs of Fallujah would eat the dead mujahideen while he and his platoon lay prone in the sun for hours. They couldn't move so they stayed behind cover and watched the dogs eat the dead.

There were other stories but that one sticks out.

He was transitioning into the "normal" world and he had to leave the baggage of the war behind. And to do this he had to tell his story. Not for me but for himself. He had to tell the story to make sense of what he had been through.

▦▦▦▦

My grandfather never really talked about the war until he was over one hundred and going senile. He was pretty sharp for an old dude, but he started to slip after his ninety-ninth birthday.

Maybe my grandfather didn't need to talk like my Marine buddy. The war ended and he went from the military into a world populated by men with similar experiences. Men who understood each other. Men who went on to sculpt and mold the world.

He served as a pilot in the Indo-China theater during the Second World War. He flew cargo over the Himalayas, and back again with Chinese workers heading for the Burma Road.

The stories he told were funny. Like how he and his fellow pilots somehow got a supply of fresh beef in INDIA and opened a hamburger stand at the airfield.

Then there was the time he had too much wine at Thanksgiving dinner and told the table about the night he lost his virginity at a brothel in Calcutta. He said it was a classy place for officers only and insisted the girl was half Anglo.

According to Grandpa, the most dangerous part of the trip to China was having to spend the night in the barracks with the Flying Tigers. They were a group of rough mercenaries who were pressed into the American command structure when the US entered the war. At night they'd drink and play poker, but the games would inevitably lead to brawls and actual shootouts—in the barracks.

Later, in his advanced age, my grandfather would tell me terrifying stories about being attacked by Jap Zeros over the Himalayan foothills. After he died, I read his letters home and they were disturbingly sad: "Dear Dad, Today we were bombed and strafed. Many were injured. Jimmy got hit ..."

I became his caretaker just before his one hundredth birthday. At that time, my stepdad was about to leave on a trip to Myanmar. Grandpa kept asking, "*Where's* he going?" and I'd say, "Myanmar." He didn't get it and kept asking the question, like old people do.

Finally I realized my mistake and said, "They used to call it Bur-Mah."

His eyes lit up and he said, "Oh! I've been to Burma!"

Senility is a funny thing. The elderly can be completely confused about where they are and who's who and no, we're not in tornado country, Grandpa, we're perfectly safe, please turn off CNN. And then they can have moments of crystal clarity.

And so, with impressive recall, down to the call sign on his plane, he told me the story.

They got an emergency call from a British airfield in Burma. They were under attack by a large Japanese force and were requesting evacuation.

Grandpa and copilot scrambled and jumped into their C-47 cargo plane. By the time they got to the airfield it had been overrun. The runway was cut into thick jungle and it was covered with Jap soldiers. The Brit survivors were holding out at one end of the runway.

Without hesitation, Grandpa landed the plane. Just landed right on top of the Japs. They didn't circle and think about it. They just landed.

The plane bowled the Japs out of the way. Dead and dying Japs and associated body parts were everywhere.

They stopped at the end of the runway, turned the plane around, and the surviving Brits piled in. By this point the Japs had regrouped and were running down the runway shooting as they went. Grandpa gunned the engines and they took off right through the Japs.

They made it back to the base in Assam. The plane was full of bullet holes, and they had to clean blood and body parts out of the engines and landing gear.

I'd read Tim O'Brien by this point, and I sensed the trueness of the story from the matter-of-fact telling and lack of embellishment. And from the utter lack of a moral or meaning.

But still I pressed him to give me some sort of meaning—some sort of neat little ending.

"Did you shoot at the Japs?"

"We didn't have guns."

"Not even a pistol?"

"They didn't issue pistols to pilots."

"Did the Brits shoot out through the doors?"

"No."

"Did they cheer when you took off?"

"No."

"Did the Brits thank you?"

"I can't remember."

Then senility came roaring back and he asked, "Where's your stepfather going again?"

He had his military records in a filing cabinet in our basement. I found the commendation. He was awarded a Silver Star for his actions that day.

Later, after he passed, I related the story to my uncle. He had no idea that his dad had a Silver Star. But he understood why he never told the story. My uncle is a Vietnam vet. He has his own stories he's never told.

I don't know why Grandpa told me that story. I guess it was something he needed to say before he died. Before he moved on to the next phase.

I'll never be a war hero. I'll never use a cargo plane as a weapon and save the good guys. I'm too old. I'm too sick.

Lee Sandlin, in his essay "Losing the War" writes, "I'm old enough now that the only way I could figure in a future war is as a victim."

That's me. The best I can hope for is to be a future war victim, which isn't a pleasant thought.

However, I did try once. I tried to enlist a few days after 9/11. I had almost died from undiagnosed juvenile diabetes a few days prior. The recruiters literally laughed me out the door. So I missed out on the Global War on Terror.

In retrospect, I was damn lucky. The timing of my diagnosis was a little too perfect. The older I get, and the more I live this life, the less I believe in coincidence. And this particular coincidence is a reminder that things happen for a reason and my life isn't my own.

▄▄▄▄▄

Instead of going off to Iraq or Afghanistan I fell into the entertainment industry. By the end of 2001, I was working in broadcast sports. By September of 2002, I was working as a PA on feature film sets.

I knew nothing, but I was a hard worker and a quick learner, so they taught me The Business. And slowly I moved up.

I never saw a dead Arab get eaten by a feral dog, and I really don't want to compare my experience to going to war. But I too have stories to tell. Stories I *need* to tell. So I can work out the meaning for myself. So I can transition into the "normal" world. Because I want out of The Business. It's been more than twenty years and it's time for me to move on.

Often I tell these stories on Twitter (now called *X*).

Social media is much maligned, and maybe rightly so, but it's been good for me. It can turn into a time-suck if I let it, but overall, it's been positive. I don't get into beefs and I'm quick to block idiots. And it's nice to engage with people who share my skepticism about the people and institutions that run our world.

I've been on Twitter for a long time. Initially I used it as a news feed. I'd lurk but never engage. Every few months I'd delete the account and start over.

Then I did a funny thing. I started writing about work. And apparently people liked what I wrote because they started following me.

And the writing has been helpful as I'm trying to make sense of things. Trying to process. Trying to sort things out. I can think about something all I want, but it's not real as long as it's in my head. And even if I write it down it's not truly real unless someone else sees it.

So I get touched by the muse, write, post, repeat. If just one person likes it, I'm a) flattered, and b) know it's real. And when it's real I can file it away and move on.

Once it's out there, once it's real, I don't want to look at it again. I don't want to deal with it. Like I say, I just want to move on.

So many strange things have happened to me over the years. But then again, I'm in a bizarre business, and weird shit happens at my workplace that would never happen in any other professional environment.

One of the weirder work experiences I've had involved a famous lead actress getting ass fucked by a famous lead actor in her trailer while the whole crew was within earshot. We knew she was getting ass fucked because she kept screaming, "FUCK MY ASS!"

And that's it. That's the story.

At least, that's the gist of it. But there's a longer version. I could make that story as long as I want to make it. I could draw it out for thousands of words, like Karl Ove Knausgård telling the story of his teenage self trying to score beer in a frozen dumpy Norwegian village in *My Struggle*.

There's an infinite number of ways to tell a story, and that's true of this story.

I could talk about how hot it was that day. Or how the production was behind because the lead actor was a giant prick who would get fall-down drunk in his trailer. When he finally decided to do a scene the only way he could get out of his trailer was to sober up by snorting coke and huffing straight oxygen.

The movie was a period piece set in the 1970s. As such, all the props and set dressing were vintage. Things like the telephone on the kitchen wall. Props like that are one of a kind—you can't just find props like that anywhere.

We were filming in a house on a suburban street. The scene was the lead actor standing in the kitchen pleading with his wife over the phone—the vintage one-of-a-kind phone.

The actor flubbed a line and blew the take—he flubbed it because he'd been spending too much time partying and not enough time memorizing his lines.

He knew he had fucked up. A normal person would have apologized to his coworkers and promised to remedy the situation.

He would have promised to do better in the future. Because that's what normal people do when they fuck up at work.

But this guy wasn't normal. This guy was a celebrity. This guy had Oscars. This guy was treated like a god. And now he was angry. He was angry at himself for blowing the take. But instead of pausing and having a moment of self-reflection, he decided to take his anger out on the world.

Ancient gods would throw lightning bolts to express displeasure. All this guy had was a vintage corded house phone.

So he took the handset of the vintage phone prop and smashed it into the receiver. He smashed it over and over again. Vintage plastic was flying all over the set. When the handset finally fell apart he ripped the receiver off the wall and smashed it on the floor. Then he picked up the pieces, stormed off set, found the prop guy, and demanded he fix the phone or be fired.

The prop guy, stoically and dutifully, took the broken phone to the prop truck where he urgently glued it back together. The phone looked perfect—like nothing ever happened. Like it never had a run-in with an angry Oscar winner. We were shooting again within an hour.

Anyway, it was hot that day. We were shooting at the same house. I can't remember if this was before or after the phone incident, but it was the same week. I was a PA. My job was to do whatever random tasks the assistant directors needed me to do. On this particular day, my job was to stand on a suburban street next to the lead actor's Star Waggon. I was supposed to radio the assistant directors when the drunk and/or high lead actor stepped out of his trailer to come to set.

But the lead actress was there that day too. They were having an affair. A very public affair. And judging by the noise it was quite passionate.

I, and everyone else standing near the trailer, could hear it. Eyebrows were raised. Glances were exchanged. Then we all drifted away from the trailer. Some epic fucking was going down.

He was absolutely wrecking her. The trailer was rocking, visually *and* audibly.

She was screaming in approval and shouting for more.

The first assistant director (1st AD) came on the walkie and demanded to know what was taking so long. I didn't know what to say. I think I replied with, "Uhh, he's busy."

The response on the radio was, "Busy with what?"

The director was antsy. He wanted to shoot. The director of photography (the camera guy, known as a DP) was antsy too. The light was perfect, but the sun was moving. They needed to shoot the scene *now*.

Again I heard the same question, only this time with anger, "Busy with WHAT?"

The 1st AD was screaming at me over the radio. He was doing this to appease the director and the DP. It was a signal to them that he sensed their urgency and was doing his best to move things along even if it meant screaming at a lowly PA.

Still, I was speechless. I didn't want to say that our principal talent were fucking on a suburban street over an open radio channel. I'm no prude, but this was uncomfortable.

Also, there were the paparazzi. Our radios weren't encrypted and the paparazzi had scanners. They were listening to all of this. They always do. So you never use an actor's real name on the radio. You refer to him by his number on that day's call sheet.

For example, you'd say, "Number One is walking to set."

Or you'd say, "Number Two is asking Number One to put his cock in her anus."

Fed up by my lack of communication, the 1st AD stormed off the backyard set and came onto the street to find out what was happening. And then he saw me down the block, and not standing by the trailer as I had been told.

My insubordination set him off and now the screaming really started. There were a lot of what-the-fucks? and fuck-yous! Some of it was over the radio, some of it was just shouted down the street. As a general rule, when someone starts melting down and screaming, the rest of the crew gets out of the way and makes themselves scarce, so it was just the two of us on the street.

I started walking toward him, motioning for him to keep it down. I wanted to explain the situation in person so I could keep it off the walkie. But the closer I got the more he was screaming at me to get back to my post at the trailer.

Right when I got to him, right when we met in the middle of that street at the halfway point between set and the fuck-shack, is when it ended. Maybe the screaming AD killed the mood, or maybe they were just done, but right when I was about to explain what was happening and why I really really didn't want to stand by that trailer, the happy couple emerged from the Star Waggon.

They did the scene, it was great, and that was that.

Except, that *wasn't* that. At least not for me.

I had gotten trapped in an impossible situation and ended up taking the blame. In the end, the lead actress wasn't the only person to get fucked that day. I didn't get fired, but it was close.

But at least I knew what happened. At least I had a grasp of the situation. And at least I could explain it to myself. That's a story I can process.

And yet, it still bothers me all these years later. I haven't let it go.

ᗆᗆᗆᗆ

There are other stories I have trouble with. Mainly because I can't remember exactly what happened. Because of time and the booze and the drugs.

My first crush was a girl on a wildly popular TV show. I was in grade school, she was on TV. It was a prime-time sitcom. I watched the show every week just to see her. I fantasized about her, but I never thought I'd actually meet her.

But I did meet her. This was many years after the on-set ass-fuck incident. I'd worked my way up to producer by this point.

My wife, who also worked in The Business, had just completed some shitty indie movie, and we were at a wrap party in a scuzzy restaurant off Melrose. Me and my grade-school crush were both stupid drunk and made out in a corner.

Or did we? I'm really not sure what happened.

Did I make out with the actress—or did I make out with my wife, or somebody else? I really don't know.

I was drunk and high on painkillers, and she was hitting on me, touching me, had her hand inside my suit jacket. And she was slutty and nasty and had gone way beyond The Wall (past the point where a woman is no longer sexually desirable).

At one time she'd been an international sex symbol. At one time she'd had a great body. She had made a career out of it.

That was over, but she was still trying. She hadn't given up.

My wife was there and she was pregnant. And I was on the verge of overdosing on Johnnie Walker and painkillers like I was most nights. I also was wearing a black suit. But other than that, I'm not sure. It's like a dream.

Am I the type of guy who would get drunk and make out with a slutty aging actress when his pregnant wife is in the next room?

I probably am that guy. But that doesn't help me establish what happened.

Maybe I need to elaborate on this story too. I could talk about the bad music, and the cold appetizers, and how wrap parties always have cold appetizers, or how the crush of my youth locked eyes with me from across the room.

She looked at me hungrily, like I was dinner. Maybe I looked good in that suit. Maybe it was because I was there with my wife, because there's a large subset of women who are into married guys.

Or maybe I just looked vulnerable—like easy pickings. Some doable drunk guy who would make her feel good. Who would make her forget about her aging face and expanding body and vanishing career. Because she wasn't aging gracefully, and she no longer had a future in this business.

The danger of not remembering is that my mind tends to fill in the blanks in such a way that the story makes sense. For example, I'd like to say I fucked her. Because that story would make sense. Grade-school crush to drunken hookup twenty-five years later after her star had seriously faded. Now that's a story.

But that's also the *Sunset Boulevard* story, which has been remade several times over. There's a moral in that story. And it would make perfect sense if I told it.

You'd understand that story. I could connect with you over that story.

But it's not true. It couldn't be. I went home with my wife that night.

Of course the way to tell this type of story is to start with some throat-clearing about how much I love my wife and how beautiful she is and how lucky I am to have her as the mother of my children. That's all true, by the way, but it's not the honest way to tell the story.

Because the story is about me and my philandering tendencies. That's the core of the story. Everything else is just fluff. The fluff is there to keep you occupied while I slowly stab you with the real meaning.

It's sleight of hand. The best stories are told this way. The story-teller creates a diversion, and you don't even notice the knife entering your back.

For now I have to ask myself, Why do I even need to tell this story? Tact and common decency would dictate that I keep it to myself. I don't need to spread it around in a book.

Why do I feel the need to get the story out and why do I have to make it real?

I used to numb the pain with booze and pills. Now I write.

I get touched by the muse and I write.

I write to tell my story to myself. Because I need to be honest with myself.

So I'll get the stories out. I'll tell them to myself, and I'll tell them to you.

Then I'll move on.

BURDEN OF DREAMS

"Nature here is vile and base . . ."
　　—Werner Herzog

Les Blank's 1982 documentary *Burden of Dreams* chronicles the making of Werner Herzog's *Fitzcarraldo* (also released in 1982). It's an incredible film, and the only instance (that I'm aware of) where the "making of" was better than the actual movie.

Based on true events, *Fitzcarraldo* is the story of an opera fan (played by the mentally ill Klaus Kinski) who tries to build an opera house in a backwater city in the Amazon of the nineteenth century. To fund this venture he must haul a steamship over a mountain so he can harvest rubber from an unexploited tributary of the Amazon.

In the documentary, Herzog says he could have done the entire film on a Hollywood studio backlot, but instead opted to film in the Amazon for the sake of authenticity. Furthermore, he got a real 320-ton steamship and hauled it over a real mountain, again for the sake of authenticity.

Of course, this was more authenticity than was needed. The steamship of the historical Fitzcarraldo (Carlos Fitzcarrald) weighed only 30 tons. He cut it into three pieces, hauled it over a small hill, then reassembled it on the other side. But a mere 30-ton ship cut into thirds wasn't good enough for Herzog's grandiose vision, so he took a film crew, actors, and a 320-ton steamship deep into one of the harshest environments on Earth and put them through what was undoubtably months of living hell.

And to top it all off, they cast a mentally ill man in the leading role. Jason Robards was supposed to be the lead, but he became ill and was replaced by Herzog's frequent collaborator Kinski.

I call Kinski a madman, and he was (in 1950 he was clinically diagnosed with psychopathy after stalking and attempting to strangle his theatrical sponsor), but he wasn't that different from the typical "heavy" actor. Many method actors, in fact, are very similar to Kinski. They're mentally ill, unbalanced, unstable people. It's that illness and instability that makes them great actors. But for the crew it can be a hellish experience.

Imagine there's a crazy dangerous homeless man on the subway platform. He's shouting obscenities and hurling threats. You don't want to get too close because he might have a knife. And you don't want him to see you because you might become a target. So you ignore him. You move to the other side of the platform. Then your train comes and you quietly board and thank your higher power when the madman stays behind to threaten the next batch of commuters.

Now imagine you work with the homeless guy. And not only is he a coworker, but he's the most important person at your place of employment. You have to do what he says, and cater to his every whim, and take his abuse. Because if you don't take the abuse, you'll get fired. And if anything happens to him, everyone gets fired.

What would that do to you? What kind of workplace would that turn into?

One of the amazing things about *Burden of Dreams* is that one of Kinski's tantrums was caught on film. He's standing on a muddy rise viciously berating the production manager.

It's an amazing moment because while I've seen many of these exact kinds of tantrums in real life, it's very rare that they're captured on camera. (The Behind the Scenes team usually stops rolling when the lead actor starts screaming.)

I must say Walter the Production Manager (the guy who got berated) handled it quite well. I've been in the same position many times and I wasn't so nice about it. Walter stood his ground, then confidently threw it back in Kinski's face. This is the correct way to proceed. The incorrect way is to become apologetic, because when faced with a dangerous insane man you must never show fear (it's very similar to dealing with an angry moose or bear or other wild animal).

The other incorrect thing to do is to get angry and go too hard the other way. I've certainly been guilty of this. And if you get up in their face, and start making threats, then well . . . you've gone too far. I know for most red-blooded men that sounds counter-intuitive, that you're not allowed to fight back. But those are the rules. And I don't make the rules.

Once the crazed actor has found his victim the rest of the crew averts their eyes and moves away. Just like the commuters on the subway platform. There's nothing they can do to help anyway, so why stick their neck out?

I'm ashamed to say that I've done that too. I've seen my friends and coworkers abused for no good reason, and I was helpless to stop it, so I did nothing.

I'm not proud of this.

Scenes like that traumatize people. You're under so much stress, you're sleep-deprived, you're physically exhausted. And then someone starts screaming at you and you can't just punch them in the face because they're the star and you'll get fired and your career will be over.

And you can't just walk, because it's the same deal: your career will be over. So you have to suck it up.

But worse than that, you have to walk on eggshells because you're terrified it will happen again. It's like you're waiting for a bomb to go off. You know the bomb is ticking and about to blow, and you know where the bomb IS, but you can't do anything about it.

This wrecks people. Just ruins them.

It's like some sort of PTSD. A lot of people (like me) turn to drugs and alcohol to numb themselves. Other people leave The Business never to return. And they can't return. They're broken.

It's amazing to me that anyone would find this romantic. Living in some extreme environment, knee-deep in mud, working horrible hours, and you're trapped with a madman who could snap at you at any time for no reason at all.

But people are attracted to this. They think it's glamorous. I guess it's the fame factor. They want to be close to fame. To paraphrase David Mamet, they think fame is contagious and they can catch it from close contact. But you can't. Fame doesn't work like that. And I'm not sure it's something you want.

It's certainly not something I want. I don't want it because I've been close to it. I see what it does. I see how broken and sick these people are. I like my anonymity. And I like my sanity (what's left of it anyway). I know how hollow the life of a celebrity is. Some people treat them like gods, like modern-day deities living and walking among us. You know this.

But they're not gods. I know better. I've been around them long enough to know.

It took me years to deal with it, and make peace with it, and make peace with myself. Not everyone is so lucky. This kind of abuse is no joke. And you're probably not tough enough to deal with it.

I saw two assistant directors get fired at the same time. We were working on the same film, and they had been the ones who'd hired me. On the last day of prep, the day before the first day of filming, they were working at the production office. Their mistake happened at the end of the day when they were heading home.

They got into the elevator with the lead actor and introduced themselves. He had them fired on the spot for making eye contact. These things happen. It's part of the deal. It's part of what you sign up for when you agree to work on a movie.

Burden of dreams indeed.

I haven't been in a truly abusive work situation in many years. Things have changed a bit since Me Too, and that type of bad behavior is less common. But it still happens.

I'm not sure how I'd handle it if I saw that today. I'm older and somewhat wiser, but I'm also quicker to anger. I don't hold back like I did when I was in my twenties.

But again, I'm not sure what I'd do. I'd like to say I'd take him to the ground and choke him out. Because I want out of this business and I don't care about my career like I used to. And needless to say, it would be a hell of a retirement announcement.

But I honestly don't know. I don't know what I'd do.

COMMERCIAL WORLD

The TV in your home or the device in your hand isn't there to educate or entertain. It's there to sell. Paid streaming has changed the calculus a bit, but for the most part, every TV show exists solely as a vehicle to deliver advertising content.

The sum of all the ads is greater than the sum of the entertainment. Meaning, the money put into the ads—the production, the post-production, the talent fees and residuals, and (most importantly) the ad buy—is greater than the money put into the actual TV shows. The "suits" at the network put on their suits to look good for the advertisers.

To put it bluntly: there's a fuckload of money in TV commercials. This was truer in the past than it is now, but when I first got into commercials the money was just plain stupid.

After getting my start in broadcast sports I fell into movies. I worked my way from set production assistant (Set PA) up to a visual effects unit production coordinator. But I decided I wanted to join the Director's Guild of America (DGA) as an assistant director (AD).

These are people who basically run the minute-by-minute operation of a film set. A 1st AD is something like a crew chief, but he also sets the schedule. It's a hard job, but it's prestigious and lucrative.

That's what I wanted: money and prestige.

The DGA is very selective. There are a few paths in, but the most common one (and the one I chose) is getting your "days." This has changed, but at that time, you needed to work 640 days on set as a production assistant (PA) before you could apply to join. For me, it would have taken three to four years to get the days.

I was happy to take the demotion from my coordinator position and go back to being a PA (it's actually fun work), but the issue was money. PA work does not pay. It's the lowest-paid job in the industry. Even the Craft Service people (the folks who provide food and drink to the cast and crew) are union and make a decent living. PAs are on starvation wages.

The worst job in the industry is a NYC Parking PA. The city of New York does not give posted parking for film productions. So if you have a big production and need to park the trucks and trailers you hire Parking PAs. They sit in their car on a certain block, wait for a car to pull out, then they put down a traffic cone. Then they guard that cone and make sure some angry New Yorker doesn't take the spot.

They do this twenty-four hours a day (in shifts) for weeks on end. They pee in bottles in their cars, because if they step away to use a restroom someone is going to move the cone and take the spot (not to mention the impossibility of finding a public restroom in New York City).

Set PA work isn't quite that bad. The hours are long—sixteen-plus-hour days are common—and you're on your feet the entire time. But at least you're not alone. You've got your PA brothers with you and they've got your back. There's something special about the comradery that comes from shared misery. Also, the catering is usually pretty good and there are always attractive women around.

And you learn. As a PA you learn everything. You see everything. You see how it's done and how *not* to do it (oh god, did I see how not to do it). And by the end of 640 shoot days, you're a goddamn machine. You know everyone's job and what they do and how they use their tools. You're well past the proverbial 10,000 hours that leads to expertise. You start seeing things before they happen. You are *ready*.

Sometimes, though, PAs are *not* ready. Sometimes they turn into "lifers." Guys who never move up. Sometimes they never really get it. Sometimes they burn out and lose all ambition. Often they say fuck this place and fuck these people, I'm taking dad's advice and going to law school.

I was down for the challenge. The only issue was money. I couldn't live off a PA wage. Try taking a girl out when you're surviving on ramen.

The coordinator job paid well. I was living a nice lifestyle for a twentysomething in a big coastal city. It was young-professional money, and as a college dropout, I didn't have the burden of student loans. I had a nice new truck, a cool apartment, and enough left over to take girls on expensive dates. So, if I was to get my DGA days, I had to figure something out.

Then I learned that being a commercial PA paid twice as much as a movie set PA. In fact, most wages in Commercial World are higher. They're often double or more what you make on a movie (per day at least). At that time, a feature film set PA made $90 to $100 per day. But a commercial PA made $175 to $200. It was a huge difference. A feature PA was on starvation wages, but a busy commercial PA could make $50 to $60k a year, which wasn't bad in the early 2000s.

In the world of production crews, there's a definite hierarchy. Feature film people are at the top, then comes episodic television, then stuff like three-camera sitcoms (which are almost extinct). Then it's the commercial people. And below that is music videos, then reality TV, and finally porn.

The feature people tend to look down on the commercial people. That is, until they find out how much we're making and then *they* want in.

There are a few differences, but it's basically the same kind of work. The same workflows, the same tools, the same equipment, and many of the same people. All film workers in the US generally go back and forth from movie to TV to commercial projects. The "film" in "film worker" refers to the workflow, not the final product.

But without question, commercial production is a civilized lifestyle. You're not working crazy movie hours for months on end. You go in for a day or two, make some coin, and then you're done. And you can be present in other peoples' lives—you can actually build meaningful relationships. You can fall in love and get married and start a family. That's almost impossible in movie world.

So I got into commercials. Just prior to this, I was on a movie that ran on for almost three years. Now I was doing projects that were two or three days a pop. Sometimes we'd shoot for two weeks but that was rare. It was just little short hits and I was fine with that—mainly because it was interesting work. Commercial set days still counted toward DGA membership, so I was able to keep moving toward my goal of becoming a 1st AD.

On a movie you can be stuck on stage for months. Most of a movie is dialogue, so it's just actors on set talking. The action scenes and car crashes are mostly 2nd Unit. So if you're on 1st Unit it's mainly dialogue (yawn).

I had come from doing visual effects (VFX) work, which entailed months of tedious technical work shooting elements in front of a green screen. Most of the day was just programing the motion-control arm. It was boring. Mind-numbingly boring. To this day when I see that chroma green color of a green screen I start to fall asleep.

But commercials weren't like that. Every day was different. We were always doing car chases or comedy stunts or blowing shit up—the fun exciting stuff.

I also got to do more stuff on set. On a union movie set you're not allowed to touch anything. It's a job security issue. You can't touch a stinger (extension cord) because that's the Electric Department's job. You can't touch a director's chair because that's the 3rd Prop Assistant's job. You can't even pick up trash because that's Craft Service's job.

The commercial sets were union too, but the rules were more relaxed. For example, on a film set I could not drive a truck—that was for Teamsters only—but on a commercial set I could. So I would drive to J.L. Fisher and pick up the dolly. I would pick up all sorts of stuff. Any and every piece of specialized prop or equipment. I picked it up and loaded it into my truck. I got to play with all the toys.

The day would start by picking up the truck, usually at Galpin in Hollywood. Then I'd tool around town filling up the truck. We'd shoot for the next day or two and then I'd have a return day where I took back all the stuff I had picked up.

One day a PA buddy and I were asked to pick up a 5-ton at Galpin. A 5-ton is a pretty big truck—especially in the city. Today you need a Teamster with a CDL (commercial driver's license) to drive one, but back then we could handle it. The next thing on the list was moving supplies. Then we were off to a series of design stores in West Hollywood. Neither of us was union Art Department, and we shouldn't have been handling set dressing, but we were getting paid and having fun and racking up our DGA days so fuck it.

Once the truck was loaded with what might have been a million dollars' worth of designer furniture we called the production coordinator and asked where we should take it. She gave me the address of a house up in The Hills. Which was odd, because I didn't remember that on the shooting schedule.

We arrived at the house and we were greeted by . . . the director's wife. It was their new home, and we spent the rest of the day moving in her new furniture paid for by the production company and written off as set dressing. It was good to be a commercial director back then.

Did I mention the money? It was a cascade. Like a waterfall.

This was just before internet ads took off, when (it was thought) the best way for a brand to reach its customers was by advertising on broadcast TV. Money wasn't an object. These corporations were basically funding million-dollar 30-second art films. They wanted extravagance and we gave it to them.

And if they wanted a high-quality image, a look that was as good (or better) than a motion picture, there were only so many people they could go to. In the days before digital cine cameras, you had to shoot on film. And there were only a select few with the skills to pull it off.

With a limited talent pool and high demand, the rates for commercial directors were insane. These guys were raking in cash. I worked for one director who had a Ferrari collection. Not two or three Ferraris, but many. I'm not sure how many he had because I never saw them all.

With the money came power, and with power came ego. And with ego comes associated bad behavior. There was one director who would have his production team take Polaroids of the entire crew. They'd then put the pictures into a binder. When the director wanted to fire someone (because of perceived incompetence, insubordination, or just because he was in a shitty mood), he'd flip through the binder and point to a picture. Firings were a daily occurrence on his sets, though because he didn't have the balls to fire someone to their face, he'd make somebody else do it.

I heard an anecdote about one of his firings. A brand-new PA was tasked with saving the director a parking spot near the stage. The director arrived, and not knowing what the director looked like or what he was driving, the PA politely told him that this spot was saved for the director and he needed to park somewhere else. The director did as he was told, found another spot in the lot, then walked into the stage and ordered his producer to fire the kid.

Many of these top-tier commercial directors liked to party. One was notorious for coming into the production office and taking all the petty cash. We called it "petty cash," but it wasn't a petty amount. It was all the cash required for crew per diems, fuel for vehicles, purchasing props and wardrobe, and any other random thing that came up. In those days a typical commercial production could go through upward of $50k in cash.

So this director would come into the office and raid the petty cash. Then he'd shack up with some hookers and a pile of cocaine, only returning when the money ran out. The production team would then have to cover for it. Why? Because the director had all the power and they did not. They wouldn't dream of sending him a bill because he'd just fire them. So they'd bring me in at wrap to photoshop fake taxi receipts. And let me tell you, it takes a long time to create $12k in counterfeit taxi receipts.

That same director was a bona fide genius. He made his career directing grunge music videos in the 1990s. By the time I met him in the early 2000s, it was all private jets and cocaine.

His sets were a performance unto themselves, and he was the star of the show.

The team would get ready for him hours in advance. He had to have his special cooler with Evian water and Jack Daniel's standing by. All the PAs would receive a pack of Marlboro Reds and a lighter, with instructions to put a cigarette in his mouth and light it should he approach.

Then, after letting the anticipation build and the clients wondering where the fuck he was, he'd burst onto the set like Elvis. He'd rip off his leather jacket, the camera assistants would put the camera on his shoulder, and he'd go at it.

Another thing he was known for was throwing cameras. After he'd get a shot and was happy with the results, he'd do his own special mic drop. He'd take the Arri 435 camera—which weighed about forty pounds and cost a half-million dollars—and just pitch it straight up into the air. Then he'd turn and walk away as his camera assistants scrambled to catch it.

The first time I worked for him was illuminating. He was on set having a screaming fit, railing at one of his producers. I was standing on the edge of the set, bored, so I pulled out one of his Marlboros and lit it up—not for him but for me. As he was screaming at the producer he saw me puffing away on the cigarette out of the corner of his eye. He paused, turned to me, and winked. Then he went right back to balling out the producer.

It was all for show. The whole thing. I figured it out, and he knew I'd figured it out. I never caught the brunt of his anger—because he knew I didn't give a fuck. That was the secret: do the best job you could and not give a fuck about the rest.

He always treated me well. He even taught me some things. I know he hasn't been working much post Me Too. I hear he's sober, then I hear he's relapsed. I think about him sometimes. He was a true genius. I hope he's doing well.

••••

I never joined the DGA.

I injured my back on set so they put me in the office. From there I started climbing the ladder. First to production coordinator, then to production manager, and eventually line producer. By the end I was doing head of production and executive producer work.

Along the way I'd occasionally get suckered into a film project. But I never liked it. I was never comfortable. I would dutifully do my job but I couldn't wait until it was over so I could get back to Commercial World.

Things have changed since I first started. Many of the big commercial production houses have gone under and the rest are on life support. As of this writing I hear the place where I used to photoshop receipts is having cash flow issues. They used to fly corporate; now they can't pay their vendors.

The first big hit came around 2008 with the rise of digital advertising, and not for the reasons you might think. Tools like Google AdWords suddenly made things transparent. Before that, advertisers had to make educated guesses about how many people saw their spots. And suddenly they realized that nobody was paying attention to their ads.

They were spending millions per spot and nobody was watching.

Sad.

Also during the Great Recession of 2008/2009, the ad agencies started getting rid of their broadcast teams. The teams were competent, experienced, and seasoned, and they made a ton of money. But to save money for the suits, they were replaced by lower paid "integrated" teams that did print, web, and some video work. But these new guys didn't understand broadcast work. Creating a great TV spot is different from creating a banner ad. It's not just a different skillset—it's a different *mindset*.

For example, if you're launching a web project you can keep making tweaks up to the point of delivery, and you can keep making creative changes after the product is delivered. If needed, you can do this for years.

That's not the way things work with film. All the creative decisions need to be made before you shoot. There's a point of no return where everything needs to be set, everything needs to be decided, everything needs to be *correct*. The integrated teams never understood this. As a bunch of junior producers and creatives, they were averse to making decisions. They didn't have the confidence to stand their ground, because god forbid they make the wrong decision.

They also didn't have the experience or the gravitas to talk the clients into spending large sums in exchange for great content. Early in my commercial career I was in the room for one of these pitches. The agency wanted to make creative changes and significantly expand the scope of the project. So the account guy sat down with the client and explained it in a confident, straightforward manner: here's why we need to do this, here's why it's the right thing to do for your brand, and this is what it's going to cost.

I forget the exact number, but the overage was in the low seven figures. And the client signed the overage. He signed it without question. Because he trusted the account guy and he trusted the agency creatives. That would never happen today.

These days the clients don't care about making prestigious little art films. They care about the bottom line and don't care if the work suffers. Most of them don't know what great work looks like—because most of them have never seen great work. The clients want content by the pound. And you can't make great art by the pound.

Today the smarter brands are no longer even using ad agencies. They've built their own in-house creative teams and taken the best of the former agency creatives. Instead of going to a commercial production company and paying a fortune for a coked-out director with a private jet, they produce the content themselves. And a lot of their content is pretty good.

From my perspective, it's great to work with these in-house units. There's no bullshit with these guys. And they would never put up with a showboat nightmare director. Egos like that cost money and time. They just care about making good content. It's refreshing.

Throughout my time in Commercial World I would occasionally get talked into doing entertainment projects. But compared to commercial content, entertainment work is slow and boring and I couldn't wait to be done with it. Of course there's no glamor in making TV commercials, but I would argue there's no glamor in anything when you're on the inside looking out.

As I like to say, glamor is a just a veneer. It only looks appealing from a distance. When you get up close you realize how flimsy and hollow and shabby it really is.

GOLDEN GATE

Back in the 2000s, when I was still single, I lived in San Francisco. For almost three years I commuted across the Golden Gate Bridge to a visual effects studio in San Rafael.

I saw a few bridge jumpers on my morning drives. That is, I saw people who wanted to die. Usually they'd get tackled by bystanders or the California Highway Patrol, but I saw one make it over the rail.

I don't remember what he looked like or what he was wearing, but I remember how he moved. He placed his hands on the rail and vaulted. It was swift and also smooth—like a gymnast mounting a pommel horse. He went over the rail and disappeared.

It only took a few seconds.

That's how long it takes to erase your own existence.

I read one figure that an estimated 1,400 people jumped/died on the Golden Gate Bridge between 1937 and 2012. But that doesn't account for the jumpers nobody saw.

The tides are strong under the bridge. Bodies are sucked out to sea and often not recovered. Crabs eat the remains, starting with the eyes. There's no telling how many have actually jumped.

Also, they like to jump at dawn.

I would fish down at Chrissy Field. There's this perfect little hooked jetty by the yacht club. On an incoming tide the bait-fish get trapped against the jetty and the striped bass go berserk. If you can catch an incoming tide at dawn, it's the chef's kiss. Nothing like catching a striper on the fly at dawn while you're staring at the Golden Gate Bridge.

Nothing like it, except they like to jump at dawn.

I was looking right at the bridge. And I saw something drop. I asked the guy fishing next to me if he saw it. He wasn't sure. Then we saw the flare. The cops drop a marine flare after the body. It floats on the water to make the recovery easier.

And then I cried. I sat on the jetty and fucking cried.

I saw several jumpers when I was fishing. But it was a good fishing spot so I kept going back. Life goes on for the living. . . .

Another time we were shooting in Pacific Heights. We had based the company (big trucks, talent motorhomes, etc.) in the Presidio. The 1st AD and I left base camp early to land the crew at set (there are rules about film crews in neighborhoods before 7 a.m., but we were sneaking in).

We were driving out of base camp and the AD saw the flare. We both started crying. I had to pull over.

We cried for a while. Two grown-ass men crying in a Toyota Tacoma on Lyon Street at 6:50 a.m. He had people close to him kill themselves too. We talked about that.

Then we put it aside and went to work. Because life goes on for the living.

■■■■

Pete grew up a few doors down from me. Always a rebellious kid. Not quite right in the head. He stole a Jeep when I was twelve and he was fourteen. We were close. I looked up to him.

He kept it together during high school. But he dropped off a cliff after graduation. His mom was mentally ill. Bipolar. Real bipolar, not the thing they diagnose girls with now. It ran in the family.

What I learned later is that men develop mental illness (real mental illness) in their late teens. Eighteen, nineteen years old is when it hits. Women get it later. In their late twenties, early thirties. It may have something to do with hitting sexual maturity.

Pete was living in a shit apartment, dealing weed, maybe acid too. He got busted breaking into a vending machine, then they searched his apartment and found the drugs.

The judge was old-school. He let Pete off the hook on the condition that he join the military.

During basic training the sergeant called his parents. He said Pete was having problems. He was paranoid and seeing things. Hearing voices. He came home and they did a psychiatric workup. He was diagnosed with schizophrenia.

A few days later, he walked into the hills above the city and hanged himself. A group of children on a school trip found his body.

▪▪▪▪

Another crazy thing about the Golden Gate is how it attracts people from all over the world. They buy one-way tickets to San Francisco just to jump. Europe, Asia, the Middle East, Australia, Africa... all over the world. It's an international suicide destination.

▪▪▪▪

My aunt (my mom's sister) was married with three kids. My mom was very close to her. Every day she was either at our house or we were at hers.

One day her husband left her for another woman. She checked into a hotel and overdosed on sleeping pills and booze.

My mother found her body.

60

First, though, she found the note. Then she started (frantically) calling all the hotels in the city. Eventually, after many hours, she found the hotel. They let her into the room and she found the body.

My mother was never the same after that. Family gatherings were never the same. There was always a heavy air when we all got together. It's been thirty years and I still dread our family gatherings.

We've certainly had other deaths in the family. But suicides are another thing altogether. Cancer doesn't shatter the survivors like suicide.

I don't know why that is. I don't know why suicide is special. It's a special kind of hell for everyone else.

▪▪▪▪

The creepiest thing about the Golden Gate Bridge (as far as I know) is that there's never been a documented case of someone jumping on the ocean side. They always jump on the city side.

They jump facing San Francisco, and Alcatraz, and the sun coming up over the East Bay Hills.

The other side of the bridge faces the ocean. You see the gray Pacific, and either a wall of fog or the horizon.

The ocean side faces the void. And they die with their backs to it.

I don't know why that is either.

THE CRAZY

If you want to move up in Hollywood then you have to work for The Crazies.

There are some wonderful people in The Business, but they're hard to get in with because nobody wants to leave them. The Crazies, on the other hand, are always hiring. They're always hiring because nobody wants to work for them. And so there's a lot of opportunity if you can put up with their shit.

The typical mental illness in Hollywood is anxiety disorder, but the full gamut runs from bipolar to borderline personality and includes, primarily for actors and directors, god complexes and a whole lot of good old-fashioned narcissism.

I very briefly worked for one production manager who had straight-up dissociative identity disorder (DID, aka multiple personality disorder). I never knew who I was talking to.

My first day, DID Chick asked me to complete some random task (which is precisely the production coordinator's job: random tasks). I completed it a few hours later and brought it to her. She asked, in an annoyed manner, why I had done this when there were more important things to do.

I said, "You asked me to do this two hours ago." She denied ever asking any such thing and accused me of lying. I started to suspect something was deeply wrong with DID Chick.

Another thing I noticed was that her accent would shift from SoCal to Southern Belle to Long Island. Later I figured out this was due to her multiple personalities. SoCal had made the request, but Southern Belle was accusing me of incompetence.

Of course, when you're confronted with someone this insane, part of you wonders if maybe *you're* the crazy one. Part of you thinks, maybe it really *was* my fault, because the only alternative explanation is that this woman is flat-out batshit crazy. But how can that be true when she's so well put together, so well-spoken (albeit with different accents), and employed by a large production company? After all, this place wouldn't hire a schizo, right?

(Right?)

But over the next day or so it dawned on me that she truly was insane. And I was stuck with her.

I have to say she was crafty in her insanity. She might have been bonkers, but she was also a Machiavellian genius when it came to office politics.

For example, she tasked me with hiring a PA to help the producer with the next day's wardrobe fitting. She also mentioned that the producer (who I hadn't met yet) liked to be surrounded by cute bubbly flirty girls.

Being a good coordinator, I found a nice young bouncy blonde PA who was also an aspiring actress and sent her off to the fitting. The production manager told the PA there was a chance she could get cast and advised her to wear something sexy and flirt with the producer (because it might help her get the gig).

Years later, when I worked again with the costume designer for that job, I found out that she—the costume designer—had been dating the producer at the time. In fact, they had just moved in together and DID Chick was not happy about the situation. So, in a very crafty evil-villainess way, she had set out to create discord in their relationship.

And I unwittingly helped.

Simply amazing.

I only lasted a few days. I think I started on a Tuesday and quit on a Thursday.

I mean, I didn't actually quit. You're not allowed to "quit." In twenty-plus years in The Business I've only said the Q-word a handful of times. So instead of "quitting," I faked a family emergency and made up some bullshit about my mom and cancer.

DID Chick freaked the fuck out—or at least one of her personalities did. I think it was SoCal. And SoCal also suffered from borderline personality disorder (BPD) and BPDs don't like to be abandoned.

She went red in the face and was crying and screaming, "How can you do this to me?" and "I will ruin your career!" and other assorted threats. Then she overturned a desk and started throwing binders and staplers and everything else within reach. Other people in the production office came to see the commotion. But no one intervened. This likely wasn't the first time they'd watched DID Chick throw a tantrum.

When she was done with the hysterics she sat at her desk crying and hyperventilating. My mouth was agape. I silently gathered my things and left. I had no response, no farewell retort.

I never heard from her again, and I have no idea if she went out of her way to blackball me, but I never got paid for my 2.5 days in her office.

So how does a woman like DID Chick stay employed? For one thing, she was actually good at her job, and maybe her multitasking multiple personalities helped her in that regard. But the bigger reason was that she was attractive. Or rather, she was hot—smoking hot. She could have been a model.

If she were an unattractive woman, she would have been in prison or a mental institution. If she were a man, she would have been shot by the police a long time ago.

If you've never seen a borderline personality tantrum, it's terrifying. Imagine a toddler having a meltdown but it's a mature adult with the capacity to inflict physical trauma.

But she wasn't a man, she was a hot woman. And as such, she stayed gainfully employed.

She's still out there, by the way. She's producing now. Mostly commercial stuff. Nothing impressive, but she's still working. I recently saw her post something on a Facebook producer's group.

I hope she got help, but somehow, I doubt it.

━━━━

DID Chick was an extreme case, but not *that* extreme. The Crazies were everywhere.

I'd be talking to a colleague and ask, "How's it going with so and so?" And they'd respond, "He's got The Crazy," and that was all I needed to know.

Often the behavior was a function of power and ego. We all have our own peculiarities, insecurities, and neuroses, but most of us are self-aware and keep them to ourselves.

For example, I'm afraid of clowns. It started the day Grandpa took me to the circus when I was five, and the fear extends to drag queens (who are very clown-like). But I keep it to myself. Mainly because it's embarrassing. I don't want someone to tell me "don't be so silly, it's just a guy in makeup," because I'm a grown-ass man and grown-ass men aren't supposed to have clown phobias, and being afraid of drag queens isn't allowed in polite society.

But when you get to a certain level of power and status no one will tell you you're being silly. And they won't tell you not to scream at your assistant for things out of their control. When you have power and feel like screaming you can just scream.

I was working on one of the old studio lots in Hollywood, a place where they used to make movies but now it's mainly offices. I was outside having a smoke and an executive was walking to his car. We both looked up at the same time to see news helicopters hovering over the Cahuenga Pass. This is the main route from Hollywood to Burbank and it's a compete nightmare if there's an accident, police activity, etc.

The executive turned to me and asked what was going on with Cahuenga? This was before smartphones and there was no Waze app to tell you the best route. I told him I had no idea.

He got angry. Instant rage. He pulled out his flip phone and called someone I assumed was his assistant. "What's happening with Cahuenga?" he said. There was a pause, and then he started screaming into the phone.

"HOW THE FUCK DO YOU NOT KNOW? *HOW*?" and he went on and on laying into this poor woman. It was vicious. Like, "You miserable cunt this, and you fucking incompetent bitch that." It's scary when you experience this in person.

And then he fired her. He fired his assistant on a flip phone from the parking lot outside his office.

And if you think that's insane, check this out: he probably hired her back the next day, and she probably came back.

I never saw this guy before the incident, and I never saw him again after it. So how do I know he hired her back? Because that sort of thing happens all the time.

There was a New York–based executive producer who was notorious for that. He'd fire the entire office in a screaming rage. The staff would then go out for daytime cocktails, and a few hours later the producer would call and demand they all come back right away. It was a regular occurrence.

This behavior was permitted because not only were there crazy people at the top, there was also a pool of people at the bottom who allowed it to happen. And there were no rules or intermediary authority figures. No one to say, "Hey, that's an insane way to treat your employees."

And if the employees did talk, who would believe them? I tell these stories to people outside the industry and they think I'm making it up.

■■■■■

So why are there so many insane people in this business?

First, I think it just attracts them. It's a little crazy to think you can leave your little sheltered life and be among the famous (among The Gods!) without there being any sort of challenges or difficulties. The sane thing to do is to stay home in Nebraska and sell insurance. But that's not good enough for the people who end up in this industry. They're the people who want more. They're the people who want the impossible. They're the people who are willing to make the impossible into reality. And how insane is that?

So they're a little crazy when they start in The Business. And then, they find that they're *rewarded* for their crazy. They're rewarded for pushing their people too hard and demanding too much (demanding the impossible). And they work harder than the others, and put in longer hours, and so they move up.

Anyone who supplants them has to be even crazier. Which means things get worse with each successive generation. A vicious cycle of crazy that leads inexorably to production managers with full-blown multiple personalities.

CREATIVE DIRECTION

There was this extra. She was so beautiful. And so sexy.

We were shooting outside of LA in NorCal (Hella NorCal). The extras outside of LA are of a higher quality. In LA they're basically scum. SAG commercial Background Actors are top tier (because that shit PAYS), but it's downhill from there.

There really is a place called Central Casting (straight outta). Though it's not quite as romantic as you might think. Parole and probation officers take their clients straight to Central Casting because they'll give a job to anyone. *Anyone.* Which means you don't leave valuables sitting around when it's a big background day (a shoot day when many extras are present). These are people incapable of doing anything better than standing around all day waiting to collect fifty bucks.

But shooting outside of LA is different. You get a different class of people. These are nice normal people with careers and maybe they do a little acting on the side, like summer stock or dinner theater type stuff. Then a movie comes through town and they get asked to be background and they sign up. Most of them do it out of curiosity, but some of them think it might lead to bigger things (it never does).

This particular beautiful extra was a grad student at the local university. I forget what she was studying. She was from Denmark (did I mention she was beautiful?). She was also intelligent and insightful and seductive and graceful. But OMG her body . . .

She was flirting with me on set all day. She told me she could tell I enjoyed the physicality of my job (I was a PA at the time) and complimented my physique (I was in my early twenties and still had a physique). So I made a point to lift heavy objects in front of her. We were filming at an airport. I was doing a lockup (making sure civilians didn't walk into the shot) next to an airplane on the stairs outside the jetway.

There was a solid metal bar just above my head, so between takes I would whip off ten or so pull-ups. I was a) trying to impress her, but b) I had to exert myself physically because she made me so fucking horny and I couldn't sneak away to jerk off.

I got her phone number toward the end of the day. The next day was a down day and I had a room at a nice hotel in Hella NorCal. I started making plans about all the dirty things I was going to do to her. This was going to be a GREAT day off.

And then, after wrap, when I was in the production trailer helping the 2nd 2nd AD with talent paperwork, the director came in. He said he needed the phone number for MY extra. And of course I couldn't say, "Uh, we, like, actually have plans tomorrow," because the 2nd 2nd AD was right there, and the 2nd 2nd was my superior and I couldn't let her know I was fraternizing with the background.

Even before Me Too you weren't supposed to be hooking up with the actors. Also, sleeping with extras is viewed as the equivalent of sleeping with prostitutes and isn't a good look.

So the 2nd 2nd dug through the skins (the paperwork related to the extras). She found Miss Denmark's number and gave it to the director. He proceeded to step outside and call her. And the next thing I know he was laughing and flirting with her, and then I heard them making plans for THE NEXT DAY.

He fucking stole her from me. He'd seen me talking to her all day. He'd seen the laughing and the flirting and the exchange of numbers. He'd even *complimented* me on getting her number. He said he was impressed.

What a dick move. He broke the bros before hoes rule. Unbelievable.

It was like some sort of Greek god swooping in and snatching her from me. Zeus pouncing on a sultry nymph—my sultry nymph—and ravishing her. To be honest, I have no idea what happened between them, but the fact that I never heard from her again makes me think she got ravished and enjoyed it.

▪▪▪▪

"Godlike" might be a good way to describe directors. They certainly have godlike egos, just like all creatives have big egos.

When I say "creatives," I'm referring to, well, the people who do the creating. People like writers, cinematographers, and yes, directors. On a film set the director is the king of the creatives. The other creatives merely work for him.

And when I say "him" it's because they're usually (but not always) men. This is a leadership position, and although I've experienced many exceptions, men are generally better leaders than women.

I find it interesting that creative ability seems to come with godlike egos. Maybe it's because the act of creating is a godlike ability. Before the sixteenth century human creativity as we understand it wasn't a thing. This was because men believed the sole source of creation was God (or gods plural as the case may be).

Still, I can't help but think about the divine nature of creativity. Where does an original thought come from? Creatio ex nihilo. God made the world out of nothing. That's how the world was made. And if asked, that's how a director will tell you they came up with their creative vision.

"Vision"—another word with spiritual connotations. But if you ask a director where that vision comes from, most will answer that it comes from them. They alone create their movie or show or ad—it's all down to their staggering genius. Regardless of their religious or spiritual beliefs, they're going to take full credit.

But of course they have to take the credit. Imagine I'm on some panel discussion at a film festival and I'm asked, "So Rambo, where did you get the idea for this wonderful film?" I can't say, "It was an act of divine inspiration, of which I'm a mere conduit."

I mean, I absolutely could say that, but people are going to think I'm batshit crazy and a studio is going to be apprehensive about trusting me with their film. So I have to take the credit. "The vision was all mine," I tell them. But I have no idea where it really came from. One moment it wasn't there, the next moment it was. Because that's how creativity works.

But it's not enough to merely have a vision. Every idiot film nerd has a vision. A director also has to execute his vision—the director has to take an idea and make it real. That's the hard part.

▪▪▪▪▪

I did a bit of directing over the years, but the transition didn't stick. Directing isn't easy and I didn't have the stomach for it. It's not just something you decide to do one day. It's a lot of work, and you have to pay a lot of dues.

I did a short film. Then I wrote/directed a pilot that didn't get picked up. The process was horrific.

It started when I tried to create a website/portfolio of my producing work. This was early Obama era, before Wix and Squarespace when you needed some skills to make a website.

After struggling for a bit, I decided that I would never be able to design a good website. However, I could design a really *bad* website, so I set out to make the world's worst website.

I made it look like the World's First Website circa 1997. I drew heavy inspiration from *Fat Chicks in Party Hats* but used gifs of faux Native American spiritual bullshit and wrote about how the wolf is my Spirit Animal and how I draw my producing prowess from the "Power of the Wolf." And how most producers drive Audis but I drive a Toyota because the wolf told me it's okay to drive a Toyota. And in no way, shape, or form did I talk about any of the projects I worked on or anything relevant to my experience or skillset.

It was funny. I uploaded it and sent it to a few friends with a "hehe, look what I did" note. My friends passed it on and in less than twelve hours it had gone viral and crashed the server. I freaked out and deleted the page.

I regret not putting any sort of analytics on it (hit counter!) so I'll never know how many people saw it.

However . . . a few days later I got an email from a Big Media Conglomerate. One of the execs had seen my World's Worst Website. They were launching a new Funny Or Die/Adult Swim–type network and asked me to submit a pitch for a show.

They liked my pitch and gave me funds for a pilot. It wasn't much but I pulled in every favor I had and we made it happen. I was very proud of it. I mean, this show was SO FUCKING FUNNY, and everyone who saw it thought it was so fucking funny. It was absurd and very blue and a little racist and homophobic (but in a funny way!). Think *Tim and Eric Awesome Show* or *Million Dollar Extreme*.

But when I screened it for the network execs they didn't think it was so fucking funny. They didn't think it was funny at all. One younger guy in the back of the room started chuckling, but when he realized he was the only one, he caught himself and bit his lip. Aside from the initial chuckles in the back row, there was complete silence. Eventually, maybe ten minutes in, Executive Bull Dyke Boss said, "Thanks, I think we've seen enough."

Then there was a Q&A session. Their real question was what the fuck did you spend our money on, but they didn't ask this. Instead they asked me questions about the absurdist jokes. And me, stunned and panicked like the rookie I was, tried to give them an intellectual defense of absurdist humor (thus ruining the joke and digging myself deeper into the hole).

What I should have done was throw it back in their faces. "Did you lazy fucks not read my pitch deck? Because this was all in the pitch deck. And in the scripts. And the boards. And also, fuck you."

L'esprit de l'escalier. Oh fucking well.

Oddly enough, they reached out a few weeks later and asked if I could somehow spin the concept into (wait for it) a reality-based game show because they needed a reality-based game show.

And I'm like, how the fuck do you expect me to turn this into a reality-based game show? They said I was the creative and I should be able to figure it out.

I could go on, but in short: the process broke me. I thought I had created the funniest show ever and instead of accolades I got ambushed with rejection. Rug pulled. Left disoriented. It broke me. I wasn't able to attempt another creative project for many years. (I'll stick with producing thank you very much!)

Of course, it wasn't their fault, they were just being their normal network executive horrible selves. This was my failure. Because I didn't have what it took to face down severe rejection and move on. It was a question of resiliency, and I didn't have it.

Because I'm not built that way. Because I think of myself as a mere mortal. Because I'm fallible and I'm aware of my fallibility. And I feel responsible for my own failings. If I can't bounce back from rejection, it's my fault. If I can't communicate my vision and transform it into a piece of media that the so-called managerial elite can understand, then that's my fault too.

But I have other ways to communicate. Other ways to express myself.

Directors, on the other hand, *are* built differently. And by "directors" I mean the ones that make it. The ones who get to make big movies. The ones you've heard of. There are people who call themselves directors, and people who actually do a little directing (like me). But a *real* director is a different breed.

First off, they're passionate about their work. I mean, passionate in a way that most people would not understand. It's a passion that often crosses over into obsession. An obsession that is maniacal and often self-defeating.

Maybe you've heard stories of directors doing three hundred takes of the same shot until the actors break down and threaten to quit. I've seen this a few times in person. It's not pretty. Any objective observer can see that the director is NOT going to get that exact thing he wants and no amount of takes will fix that. And nobody can tell him "no." Not the 1st AD or the unit production manager (UPM) or the executive producers.

He has a vision and is driven to achieve it and nobody is going to stop him. He'll put relationships at risk. He'll put lives at risk (happens all the time). Because he's obsessed beyond all rationality.

But then again, you need to be obsessed. Making movies is hard. And making a good movie is really really hard. And if you've never worked on a film set you will never know how hard it is.

Just know that Murphy's Law rules the day and everything that can go wrong will go wrong. And so you have to persevere. You have to push through.

∎∎∎∎

This is where the godlike ego comes in. Directors need something that tells them, "I am right and you are wrong and my pilot is really funny so go fuck yourself." They need something that tells them it's okay to do three hundred takes because they are right to do three hundred takes because it's not perfect yet. Their large ego helps them to survive. They couldn't succeed without it. It's absolutely necessary—even though it makes everyone else's lives a complete nightmare.

And the guy without an ego, well, he's not going to make it. (He probably spends his days writing books about himself.)

It's a common misconception that Great Directors are also impressive people. Sometimes they are (Michael Bay comes to mind), but more often than not they're insecure and introverted and fairly boring. Now, they're good at their jobs, and they can be fascinating when they're talking about film, but they're certainly not larger-than-life figures. They're just introverted nerdy guys.

And when you take an introverted insecure nerdy guy, the kind of guy who got picked on in high school and didn't get laid until he got to Hollywood, and then you give him a little bit of power, and then you couple that power with obsession and a giant ego . . . well, watch the fuck out.

This is especially true of animation directors. They're extra nerdy, extra introverted, extra obsessed. And then they get a taste of success and they set out to get revenge on everyone who picked on them and rejected them and didn't understand their genius. The ego and obsession spirals and they become cruel and vindictive. It's almost a rule with animation guys.

Yet a funny thing happens when a director gets to the tippy top of their game. After they've had success and they're a household name they actually become very nice people. There's still an ego, and they're still obsessed, but goddamn if they're not nice about it. When there's nothing left to prove and they can do any project they want, then suddenly they become . . . happy.

It's a strange thing.

But the director, no matter how successful, still has trouble interacting with reality as you or I know it. They can't hack it. They're misunderstood and alone. So they imagine their own reality—how things should be. And they become obsessed with making that reality into something tangible, something they can show people. Something that shows the emotions and beliefs and pain and suffering and hate and triumph and love that they otherwise can't express, that they otherwise can't emote, that they otherwise can't communicate.

So they make a movie.

This is the root of Cinema.

This is the root of all great art.

SLEEP

P eople don't understand how long filming takes. Pedestrians will pass by a set and stop to watch. They'll stick around for five, ten minutes. Then they get bored. Because very little happens on a set in ten minutes. And then they leave in a huff as if we wasted their time somehow.

It takes a lot of time to make high-end content. As a result, the hours are brutal. That's something else normal people don't understand.

For me, a typical shoot day is sixteen hours. That's eighty hours a week. I do this week after week. It takes a toll, and I don't know how long I can keep it up.

▪▪▪▪▪

Back when I was a PA, I was asked to drive a feature film art team to a tour of the French Laundry.

I picked them up at SFO and we drove to Napa. Thomas Keller himself gave us a tour of the kitchen. (The kitchen from *Ratatouille* is based on the French Laundry. That's basically what it looks like in real life.)

Not only was it an awesome day and a career highlight, but I also got some great career advice from the art director riding shotgun. She started as an assistant in the 1980s. After working her way up, by the early 2000s (when I met her) she was doing nothing but very large movies.

I asked her what was the key to her success. She explained (with much humility) that she got to be who she was because she was able to handle the long hours, whereas many people she started with could not.

In other words, she got to where she was by attrition. There were people who were smarter, people who were cooler, people who were harder working, etc., but they couldn't hack the hours, so they dropped out.

And it's not just about sleep deprivation. It's hard to have a life when you work long irregular hours. And it's impossible to build a life with someone else. Eventually you start to live separate lives and drift apart.

Divorce is endemic. The common refrain is, "The Business eats marriages." It's all down to the hours.

My wife quit The Business when we had our first kid. We wouldn't be married today if she hadn't stopped.

She'd be on some TV show, and I'd be doing my things, and we'd only see each other a few hours on Sundays. And even then we were too tired to do anything fun. (Though somehow I did manage to get her pregnant. . . .)

Union Film Workers make good money. You start with a good hourly rate and daily guaranteed hours. The guarantee is usually 10 hours, so even if you work 8 hours you're paid for 10. Overtime kicks in after the guaranteed hours. Hours 11 and 12 are at 1.5x the hourly. After 12 hours, it's 2x the hourly. Depending on your union and your contract, you can eventually hit 3x overtime.

Then add in turnaround penalites and meal penalties (money for going past designated meal breaks). It adds up to a very nice paycheck.

It's especially nice for a dropout like me who didn't have better prospects.

I used to be a producer (management). Now I'm union crew and make more than when I was a producer. The difference is I get paid for all the overtime.

But it's *rough*, and that money is *earned*.

On a recent Wednesday I only spent thirteen hours on set including the half-hour lunch. BUT it was a two-and-a-half-hour drive to set each way so that made for an eighteen-hour day. Then the next day (Thursday) I had to start at 11 a.m., but I didn't get home until 6 a.m. on Friday morning. Later that Friday, I left the house at 3 p.m. and got home at 7 a.m. Then on Saturday night, I had to leave the house at 2 a.m. And so on.

Sleep deprivation is funny. You feel like you're floating. You walk and don't feel your feet hitting the ground—but somehow you're in motion. Simple tasks become difficult. It's hard to remember names. And sometimes inexplicable things happen. Like the time I got home from a very long day, took a shower, and found a spent ZYN pouch stuck in my pubic hair. How did that get there? And how did I not feel it?

■■■■

I recently worked with a bunch of city cops. I felt like a pussy when they talked about their hours. Many of them showed up for our shoot after working a twenty-four-hour shift.

One of the cops even handed out Adderall to the other officers. I joked that I wanted crack. He said it would be easier to score meth in that part of town.

Love the dry cop-humor. . . .

▬▬▬▬

Driving home can be scary. I've fallen asleep a few times over the years. Thankfully my new truck alerts me if I'm nodding off. I hate the nanny-state bullshit in new cars but I actually like this feature.

Coming home early one recent morning on the freeway I didn't exactly fall asleep, but I was in a daze. I snapped out of it and had no idea where I was. How long had I been driving? Where was I? Did I miss my exit? How far did I go?

My worst drowsy driving experience (worse than the time I went off the road) happened on a shoot in the desert outside Palmdale. This was back when I was a PA. At the end of the night my job was to drive the film to the lab in Burbank.

I left the set at about 3:30 a.m. after working almost twenty-four hours. I remember it was raining on the 14 freeway and then cut to . . . me waking up in my truck. It was noon. The heat of the sun blasting through the windshield was what woke me up. It was HOT in that truck. I had no idea where I was.

It turned out I was in the parking lot of Fotokem in Burbank. Somehow I had driven to the lab, dropped the film, then passed out in my pickup.

Back then they would give you a receipt when you dropped the film (like a dry cleaner ticket) and I still had it in my hand. That's how I know I dropped the film.

I had no recollection of what actually happened. I checked my truck for blood/damage in case I killed someone. Thankfully it was clean.

Suddenly waking up in a strange place is very disturbing. It's a major panic moment. Blackout drunks and film workers know the feeling. . . .

You can only do so much caffeine. Years ago I was on a movie set and basically overdosed on Red Bull. I had a seizure. They took me to the ER in an ambulance.

I was having trouble walking. I needed a cane to keep from falling. Over the next week I was bounced around from specialist to specialist. Finally I saw a neurologist who fixed me.

He said caffeine strips you of potassium, as does insulin (I'm a T1 diabetic). He said I basically had a severe electrolyte imbalance. Said he sees it all the time—mostly in marathon runners and people who do fasting cleanses.

He gave me a can of V8 juice, which he kept on hand for just these occasions. It had enough sodium and potassium to snap me right back to normal, and I walked out of there without the cane.

So I keep little cans of V8 in my truck for long days. Right next to the emergency Sugarfree Red Bull and 5-hour ENERGY shots. NOTHING tastes worse than warm Sugarfree Red Bull. And chasing it with a warm V8 doesn't help.

I don't do speedy drugs (never liked them). Lately I've been taking 300mg of psilocybin to keep me awake for the drive home, but it's hard to get the timing right. Sometimes it doesn't kick in until after I get home.

█████

But here's the awesome part of night shooting: You *own* the city.

On a recent shoot we had the police department shut down six square blocks in the middle of the Big City. We broomed out the homeless and the club kids and the hoochie mamas and the city was all ours.

There was a moment where I stood in the middle of a major intersection that was completely quiet and void of life except for me and my coworkers. No traffic, no horns, no screaming homeless. Just quiet. It was glorious.

I put a chair in the middle of the street and drank my Red Bull. And when I drove from base camp to set, I ran all the red lights because I had a police escort, not unlike a president coming to town. It's the *only* way to travel in the Big City.

Places like that are beautiful when there's no one else around to fuck it up.

And on that shoot, the city was *mine*. All night long.

UNDER THE SILVER LAKE

A friend asked me to write about *Under the Silver Lake*. Initially I didn't think I had much to say about it. But it turns out I do.

The story reminds me of a time in my life that I'd mostly forgotten and that I'm mostly unable to remember. I was there but it was like a scaryish dream. Not quite a nightmare. Maybe an unhappy dream?

David Robert Mitchell's *Under the Silver Lake* (*UTSL*) is a neo-noir mystery set in 2011 East Side LA. Andrew Garfield plays what I assume is a burned-out young actor. He maybe did a few pilots but they never went to series and his phone stopped ringing.

At the beginning of the movie, he's spun into a nihilistic drift. His girlfriend has left him, he can't pay his rent, and his Mustang is about to be repossessed. He spends his time day drinking, fucking needy actresses (always a mistake!), and he "might" be killing dogs. Then one day he meets a girl at his apartment's swimming pool. They connect, but she rapidly and mysteriously disappears, plunging him into a rabbit hole of conspiracy and secret messages hidden in pop culture.

▪▪▪▪▪

My wife and I had sold our West Side house at the peak of the housing bubble and were renting a loft in Downtown LA. 2008 was a busy year, but by 2009 the Great Recession was in full swing. I was out of work for sixteen months straight. And though you don't realize these things right away, I also had a serious drug problem.

The Hollywood unions have their own health-care system, known as MPI.[1] They have their own clinics, a nursing home, and even used to have a hospital in the Valley (with union-subsidized plastic surgery for fading actors—not joking). Very well-funded, nice facilities, low copays.

I went to the Westwood clinic. I liked my doctor. He was pragmatic. And he wasn't stingy when it came to prescribing narcotics. If I had a cold, he'd give me Vicodin so I could "rest and breathe." Not one or two pills, but a bottle of thirty.

But MPI had weird rules. Wardrobe and production staff were not allowed to receive benzos. Those jobs were too stressful and most people got hooked. You had to go outside of MPI if

---

1   MPI is short for MPIPHP, or the Motion Picture Industry Pension & Health Plans.

you wanted that. It was still covered by the plan, but the copays were higher.

Hollywood was stupid permissive. At one production company where I worked there was a floating bottle of random pills. Having a bad day? Someone would give you the bottle: Xanax, Percocet, Dexedrine. It was a stressful job with long hours. Sometimes you worked for horrible people. Sometimes you needed help.

Everyone understood. Nobody judged.

Coke was frowned upon in my circle (I never really liked it anyway). But booze, pills, and a little weed were socially acceptable.

So in 2009 I was out of work. With nothing better to do I started training for randonneuring cycling events (ultra-distance cycling). I was hoping to do a 1,200 km.

Unfortunately, I trained the wrong way. As I later learned, the correct way is to do short rides during the week and do one long ride on the weekends. This way, you gradually increase the length of the big ride every week. Instead I trained by doing sheer mileage. I was riding 500+ miles a week and it was too much.

Rather than being primed for randonneuring season, I ended up with knee and hip problems. I was afraid of surgery, so my doc thought it would be best to give me painkillers.

As advertised, painkillers WORK. They make the pain go away. Then you build a tolerance and need more. Doc supplied, no problem there.

Funny things can happen, though. While you build tolerance for the pills, you lose tolerance for pain. I would stub my toe and it felt like I was dying. And though it took a while to figure out, I eventually realized I couldn't tell the difference between pain and withdrawal symptoms. Withdrawal hurts—in a very real physical way.

My wife was then working on a popular TV show, so we had money coming in. Rent was reasonable. No kids at the time. Life was easy. I had no work, couldn't bike, and was high as fuck. I spent my days walking the dog and hanging at our loft complex's rooftop pool. At night I'd hit the bars and art parties of East Side LA.

Wife was working TV-show hours. I barely saw her.

Hollywood eats marriages, as I've said. With wife working crazy hours, and me not, certain issues developed. I began living a different life. Hanging out at art parties with art hoes and actresses. Day drinking at bars and cafés. And just like that, I was adrift in LA.

■■■■

Beautiful women come to LA to be recognized for their beauty and for a shot at fame. They want you to want them. They need you to need them. They're dangerous.

UTSL has a lot of fun with esoteric messaging and film nerdery. The Easter eggs (the hidden messages embedded in the film) are fantastic. Fireworks are morse code, T-shirts have secrets meanings, and on and on.

Here's a spoiler: our protagonist discovers that all of pop culture is a construct designed to attract beautiful women to Hollywood so that rich men can be entombed with them for eternity.

━━━━━

I struggle with the question of why this entertainment-industrial complex exists. I'm writing this book partially as a way to work it out for myself. Because when you dig in, it makes no damn sense. Maybe it's starting to. . . .

I never "dreamed" of working in Hollywood. Both of my parents were in the biz but I wanted nothing to do with it. I wanted to start a construction business. First I dropped out of high school, then I dropped out of college. I became a ski-lift mechanic. Then I started building ski lifts.

On the job I learned how to do concrete and carpentry. Then I got diabetes and could no longer do physical labor.

That's when I fell into The Business, and everything clicked. I was good at the work. Like I was made for it. And I saw opportunity. There was a clear path to advancement, a ladder I could climb.

And not having dreams of fame really helped. It gave me a clear-eyed view, allowed me to go in without preconceived notions or false expectations. When faced with a reality that conflicts with their core identity, most people go into denial, and some go off the rails entirely.

▪▪▪▪

One of my best friends is an actor. Actually he's a great comedy actor, which I would argue is the highest form of acting. Good-looking guy, great chops, excellent work ethic. Unfortunately, when he was coming up, he looked exactly like a younger version of Michael Douglas. He'd go to audition after audition and hear, "You're great, but you look too much like . . ."

He had famous director/producer friends, but they could only do so much. He finally had to face the realization that he was never going to make it, and he went off the rails with the three Ds: drink, drugs, divorce.

He was living in his car for a while.

But with me, I knew it was bullshit from the start. I figured out very quickly that glamor is highly subjective, and there's no glamor when you're on the inside. On my second movie I spent a night in a hotel suite putting drugs up my nose with Oscar-winning actors. It was hands down the most boring night of my life. Famous actors are interesting when they're talking about acting, but other than that they're really fucking boring. I never sought that kind of experience again (although it happened from time to time).

Instead I just threw myself into my work. Because I loved the work. I loved (and still love) the process of creating something from nothing.

I wasn't the best, and I wasn't the smartest, but fuck I was a hard worker. I was the *hardest* worker (I still think this, by the way).

Then one day there was no work and I was cast adrift. I didn't think I'd be famous, but I always thought I'd be useful.

And then I was no longer useful.

●●●●●

I don't remember much of that year-plus of unemployment. Though I do remember that I walked the dog a lot. LA is very walkable when you don't have much to do. I did it in an opiate daze. By the end they were giving me oral morphine. All the morphine I wanted. All that I *needed*.

I made friends with the dealers and hoes in Downtown LA. They liked my dog and my dog *loved* them. Never had to buy on the street though.

Just walking around. Me and the dog and the stink of uselessness.

●●●●●

In *UTSL*, our protagonist finally finds the girl. She's been entombed for eternity under the iconic Hollywood Sign. But she's happy. This is what she's been working toward: godlike immortality.

She's achieved the goal of every beautiful woman who moves to LA. She's made it. She's become immortal. She's met her fate and she accepts it. Now our protagonist has to accept his fate.

I was hiding pills all over the loft. Was terrified that someone would take them. I always had a large supply on my person. But just in case, there were extras in my sock drawer and under the mattress and in the freezer and taped to the lid of the toilet tank. I forget how much I was taking, but I was blitzed all the time.

One day, while I was frantically trying to find my stash, I realized I had a serious fucking problem. It hit me hard: *what was I doing?*

Working with my doctor I was able to step off the pills over the course of four months. Near the end of my opiate addiction I finally went back to work. Cortisone injections and knee surgery fixed the problem.

But something was broken inside me. I think I'm still trying to fix it.

After the layoff, I went back to work with more drive than ever. Bigger and better projects. More responsibility and more money. My wife got pregnant. We left LA for flyover country. She stopped working to stay home with the baby. That saved our marriage. That and no more hot girls by the pool.

There's a dissatisfaction that comes from chasing goals—from striving. You finally get to the place you want to be and discover there's nothing there. It's empty.

I used to be into mountaineering. I was a peak bagger. The game is to "bag" (climb) as many peaks as possible. Much of it is technical climbing (with ropes, protection, etc.). It's hard work. The last time I got to the top of a mountain, I was cold and dead tired. I realized it was freezing and windy and barren at the top of a mountain, nothing but a bunch of rocks, and I wondered why the fuck I was there.

I stopped climbing after that.

I worked hard in The Business. And I got to the top of what I did. But it was cold and there were a bunch of rocks. I decided to take a different path—same industry, but different capacity.

I still fear being without purpose—of being adrift. Yet I'm tempted to burn it all down. Because purpose means responsibility, and responsibility can be a prison. I'd prefer to be free.

In *UTSL* the protagonist feared being homeless. Of being a bum. Of being somebody that no one cared about. But it's only when he's finally evicted from his apartment and has lost everything, and has in fact finally become a bum, that he finds happiness.

I think about that quite a bit. I've worked very hard for what I have. But sometimes I wonder if I wouldn't be better off if I lost it all.

I mean that in the literal sense. Lose it all. Job, wife, kids, house. All of it.

The temptation to burn it all down is always there. It's omnipresent. I can't shake it.

I've been out of LA for over a decade now, living in this beautiful mountain state. Sometimes I find myself driving around our town at night. It's usually a late-night nicotine run.

I'll be driving home from the gas station with my nicotine pouches and some great song will come on Spotify and I don't want to stop driving. Then I wonder how far I can go with the gas I have in the tank.

Not that it matters. I can always buy more gas when I run out. And when I run out of nicotine pouches, I can get more of those too. So how many days or weeks can I drive? How far can I make it?

Years ago I watched an interview with Beirut hostage Edward Austin Tracy. He was kidnapped by Shiite terrorists and held captive for almost five years. He said he dealt with his years of confinement by taking long imaginary drives.

I do the same thing on my late-night nicotine runs. In my mind I leave our small town and cross the Rockies beneath the starlit, moonless sky. Come dawn, just as the sun is cracking over the horizon, I hit the vastness of the Great Plains, and I just keep going.

Have you ever driven alone through the Plains? Once I was alone in Nebraska's Oglala Grasslands. I must have been the only person for forty miles. Driving alone on gravel roads over green hills. It was like being alone on the ocean and the grassy hills were like waves.

The last battles of the Indian Wars were fought here. They killed Crazy Horse here. He was another man who wanted to be free. They offered him a life of comfort, but it was comfort in captivity. He rejected it and tried to escape. So they killed him.

In my mind I keep driving. Past Oglala, past the Pine Ridge, past the Plains.

I cross the 100th meridian, near where the Plains end and the eastern forests begin. I cross the giant rivers of the Midwest. I pass through broken ruined former industrial towns. I eat at diners and talk to the truckers. I sleep in the truck and shit at highway rest stops.

I stop at roadside attractions. I've been to some of these places and I return in my imagination. I stop at Wall Drug and take a selfie with the giant jackalope. I stop to see the world's largest boot in Red Wing, Minnesota.

Eventually, though, my imagination fails me. Because now I'm driving through places I've never been. What are the roads in Upstate New York like? Do they have the tolls where you throw change in a basket?

Can I make it to the edge of the continent? To Maine? To Nova Scotia? Could I really make it to Nova Scotia? I've never been to Nova Scotia. I'm not sure how one gets there in a car.

I know I could get there. But I'd burn it all down in the process. Work would wonder where I was. The kids would be devastated. My wife would be beside herself. And then when she figured it out, she'd empty the bank accounts. I have credit, but eventually the finance company would come looking for my truck.

Would I be free by the time they repo my truck somewhere in Canada?

Could I make a new life for myself? Find a new purpose? Do I even need a purpose? Isn't merely existing good enough?

But these questions are moot. Because I never make it out of town. Because I never cross Rockies and head for the Great Plains.

Instead I go home.

Back to my house and my wife and my kids and the dogs and my job and everything else. Back to everything that keeps me tethered.

Back to the people and the place I love. Because even though I want to run, I still love them.

So I go back to the thing I call "my life."

PATRONIZE ME

There was a director I knew. He was a real luminary of animation. One of the Grand Masters. Respected by everyone. You've seen his movies. You loved his movies.

I know this because everyone loves his movies. I was his assistant for a time.

Later, after I worked for him, he got a multi-picture deal from a giant media conglomerate we'll call Longhouse Studios. They gave him complete creative control and built him his own studio.

He was late-middle-aged at the time, and making those movies would have taken him to the end of his career and made him a very wealthy man.

And they would have been great movies too. And I'd probably be talking about them now if it weren't for the fact that he completely fucked it up.

Like, completely and totally fucked it up. Worst fuckup in Hollywood I've ever heard of.

I would have been there for it but the schoolmarms at Longhouse Studios thought I wanted too much money and hired a childless girlboss instead. But I knew some of the team and got the live play-by-play as the disaster unfolded.

So Luminary Director started the first movie of his new deal. He started with storyboards instead of a script. Boarded it out all himself. From beginning to end.

I saw the boards. They were fucking great. It would have been a great film.

In animation, when you have solid storyboards you don't need a script. It's all about the boards. It's actually a very smart way to do things.

But the studio suits wanted to see a script. And Luminary Director said no. You gave me creative control, he said; you built me this studio, and this is how I'm doing it. Thank you very much.

The suits needed a script because that's how they track progress. The rule of thumb is one page in the script is roughly one minute of screen time. You break the page up in 1/8ths. That's the metric—how many eighths of pages have you shot?

At the end of every shoot day the AD department creates a production report that says something like, "On July 26th we shot 1 and 2/8ths pages" and includes other metrics, like how many feet of film you shot, overtime, etc.

The production reports are reviewed every so often (sometimes daily, sometimes weekly) and that's how the studio knows if the production is going well or not.

So, the suits wanted a script—because that's how suits track progress. That's their metric. And they weren't going to adapt to counting storyboard frames instead.

Luminary Director, like most directors, had a legendary ego. I'll say that his ego matched his genius. But goddamn he had a big ego.

And because of his big ego, he wouldn't back down. He wasn't going to write a script for a movie that was already in production.

But his will was no match for the power of Longhouse Studios and their process protocols and preferred metrics. He had highly placed friends but they couldn't protect him.

And so the giant media conglomerate killed the multi-picture deal, shut down Luminary Director's animation studio, and suddenly he and his entire crew were unemployed.

This was many years ago and Luminary Director hasn't worked since. He'll probably never make another movie. And this is sad because you like his movies, remember?

Again, I wasn't there.

But *if* I had been there (and *if* they would have approved my very reasonable salary request) I would have done the following:

1. Stayed up all night and typed up a script
2. Sent the script to the suits, followed by daily production reports
3. Done all of this without Luminary Director knowing

Why? The obvious reason is to save everyone's job. But the bigger, related reason is that my role (and everyone's role) in the Hollywood Patronage System is this: Take care of the people above you, and look out for the people below you.

No matter what.

It's a crucial point. And while it's not part of the recruiting practice, we select for people who understand this. Because if you don't understand it, you won't get very far.

There's a strict hierarchy in Hollywood. But everyone, from the top to the bottom, is tied together. This means you rise and fall together. And when the people you work for do well, then you do well.

An onset electrician (lighting tech) is tied to the best boy electric, who in turn is tied to the gaffer (lighting designer), who in turn is tied to the DP (camera guy), who is tied to the director, who in turn is tied to a production company, which is tied to investors and distributors.

There's always somebody above you. At least there was always somebody above me.

For the people at the low end of the totem pole, the key thing is to make your boss look good. You're useful and helpful to him so he, in turn, can be useful and helpful to the guy above him.

The system works this way because everyone is a gig worker, and it's all about getting the next gig. And if your boss looks bad then your boss isn't going to get the next gig, and you're not going to get the next gig.

Kind of like how politicians need to win the next election so their staff can keep working.

And if one of the guys at the top looks bad, then *nobody* gets the next gig and you're suddenly sitting at home worrying about money.

The entire system runs on loyalty. And these bonds are very strong.

So strong that there are people I haven't spoken to in twenty years who (hypothetically speaking) could call me out of the blue and ask me to help remove a dead hooker from their hotel room and I'd drop my dinner fork and start speeding toward Vegas with a shovel and a bag of quicklime.

So loyalty is a strong thing. You need to be loyal to the guys above you because they provide work.

But loyalty is a two-way street. Your underlings take care of you, but you have to take care of them too. You need to reward them for doing a good job.

And the big reward is hiring them again. This is called "splitting the spoils."

Aside from being The Right Thing To Do there's a very pragmatic reason for taking care of your underlings: you need them. Because you're fucked without them, and you're only as good as your last gig.

So you need them, and they need you. You're all tied together and you all rise and fall together. And the chain is only as strong as the weakest link, and one weak link breaks the chain.

Remember this.

I don't know how prevalent this is, but in my circle we liked to use mafia jargon.

Mostly because it was fun, but also because various mafia groups already developed useful jargon for working in a patronage system.

For example, if I had a minor fuckup I would say "I lost a finger." Once you've had enough minor fuckups and you're "out of fingers," then they "whack" you (you get fired).

Or someone who had a strong nepotistic connection would be a "made man."

Another mafia analogy: my crew would compete against other crews. And when I'd score a gig it was like we hijacked a cigarette truck or robbed a jewelry store.

I'd call my guy—who'd be fucking thrilled. And he'd call his guys (fucking thrilled!), who called their guys, and we'd all split the loot.

We were all in it together. Like a mafia family. It was fucking great.

And it's *still* great. All we want is for it to keep going and never end.

Remember this too.

⬚⬚⬚⬚

While you have to constantly police the people below you from fucking up, you also have to stop the people above you from fucking up.

Everyone fades. It's happening to me and it will happen to you. I know it will happen to you because it happens to everyone.

Sometimes the people at the top used to be competent and skilled and creative, but now they're burned out, or they're drinking too much, or, like Luminary Director, their massive genius has generated a massive ego that keeps getting in their way.

Or maybe they're just way past prime and running on momentum. Objects in motion stay in motion, but only for so long.

So when they start fucking up you have to jump in and save them. Because if you don't your neck is on the line.

Because you're all tied together (remember?).

There's a great scene in François Truffaut's *Day for Night* (La Nuit américaine) when the aging actress shows up shit drunk and can't remember her lines.

The prop team sees this and realize they're about to do a ton of takes, so they frantically start cutting cigarettes so they'll be at the correct length for continuity.

And then there's my hypothetical solution to Luminary Director's beef with the suits. (Which is not entirely hypothetical because I've covered for other directors in similar ways.)

There would have been a chance I'd get fired for pulling a stunt like that. But the director fucked up, and if the fuckup wasn't mitigated somehow, then we all would have gotten fired.

And then we wouldn't have gotten the next gig and there's no more loot to split and the party comes to a screeching halt.

Because you have to make the boss look good. Or else it's over for everybody. That's how patronage systems work.

How far would you go to save yourself and your mafia crew?

What would you do if it was your neck on the line?

On June 27, 2024, Joe Biden debated Donald Trump. It was a disaster for the sitting president. I have no idea why he agreed to do it so early in the campaign.

There are plenty of conspiracies, but I think it came down to Biden's ego (which has to be huge).

Either way, his underlings should have stopped him. Even if Biden refused to back out they could have sabotaged it somehow.

But they went ahead with it anyway. It was a disaster and the Boss suddenly looked bad.

And then the chain started breaking.

The people above Biden—the donors, the media, the "establishment"—started panicking. They needed him just like he needed them, but now they could see the chain stretching. So they started talking about replacing him. "Can we mend the chain before it snaps? Can we maybe fix this? Does anybody know a good welder?"

The people below Biden saw the chain breaking too. They saw the party coming to a halt. They knew there might not be a next gig or any more loot to split.

They knew they could go down with him.

So they tried to save the crew and tried to assassinate Donald Trump.

By this point, the chain was very broken. If they would have given the would-be assassin $400 to buy a cheap Vortex 3-9x scope and some Sierra OTMs we'd be living in a very different world today.

But they didn't, and through a combination of incompetence and/or divine intervention the hit was botched.

And not only did they botch the hit, but Trump came back stronger! (What was that?)

Then the chain just snapped. It all fell apart.

The whole world saw it during Biden's Oval Office address on July 24, 2024, when he announced he was dropping out of the race. Someone had to direct him from off camera to keep him moving and engaged. He kept looking camera-right (that is, to his left), pantomiming the gestures and cadence of his handler rather than looking directly into the lens.

His people knew they were breaking a big rule of propaganda and that the Boss would look bad, but by that point they had stopped giving a fuck.

Nobody jumped in to save the president. Nobody was furiously cutting cigarettes for continuity.

But the real tell was the lack of a wedding ring.

The White House employs professional makeup and wardrobe people.

They're trained to look at an actor (or president) before he goes on camera to make sure everything is correct. Perfect tie knot, watch on the correct wrist (yes actors fuck that up), wedding ring on correct finger, etc.

They always check. Because they would undoubtedly get fired for missing something like that.

But they didn't check President Biden. Because the chain was broken.

The Boss was going to look bad no matter what.

And there was no fixing it.

LIBRARY

During my brief college career I took a second job at the university library. I thought it would be a good way to earn extra cash to supplement the income from my grocery store job. Just a few hours a week and I could do it after class and not have to leave campus.

My job was to re-shelve books. How hard could it be, I thought. I had learned all about the Dewey Decimal System in school.

I got this. No problem, man.

The first thing I learned was that they no longer used the Dewey Decimal System. They used some much more mind-numbingly boring system to catalog books.

The second thing I learned is that creepy guys like to jerk off in libraries.

They'd somehow travel to the campus, walk a considerable distance (the library was at the center of a giant campus far from the nearest parking lot or bus stop), just to jerk off surrounded by books. I caught three guys jerking off in my first four-hour shift.

I lasted two weeks at that job. The jerkoffs creeped me out, but the issue was how boring it was to shelve books. Walking around pushing a cart for hours on end in complete silence trying to find a specific place for a stupid fucking book. And the classification numbers all blurred together, which made it hard to find where the books were supposed to go, so I'd just stick them in some random spot in the stacks so my cart would be empty and I'd have an excuse to walk back to the front desk for more books and talk to the front desk girls (who wanted nothing to do with me).

Of course placing a book in the wrong place in a library of that size meant the book would be lost forever.

But fuck it. Fuck the books. Time to go see the front desk girl.

▪▪▪▪

That said, I do love books. And I used to love libraries. I learned to read in a public library.

I think it was fifth grade. I would have been about ten years old. I'd go to the neighborhood public library to escape the chaos of my home.

I could have gone home after school, but Mom would probably be crying or having an anxiety attack or freaking out over money, or there might be some guy there, or maybe she'd decide to move my bedroom again, and there might not be any food, so I'd just hang out at the branch library.

It was a nice quiet place. And it was clean. And it was safe.

And the librarians were lovely. Lovely middle-aged motherly women. I don't remember their names or their faces, but I remember the vibe. And I remember that they cared.

They cared in a way that my mother or my teachers didn't. I'm sure I wasn't the first neglected kid from a dysfunctional household they'd encountered, and they knew how to handle it. They just let me be—at first anyway.

At no point did they ever take me aside and say, "You can trust me, Rambo," and give me the hugs I didn't get at home. No, that didn't happen. This isn't that story. But one of them did teach me to read.

I would look at the picture books. Anything with pictures. Anything to keep me occupied. Illustrated history books were great. I loved the drawings and photos of edged weapons and guns.

Most days I'd be in some corner with a pile of books, and the librarians would check up on me from time to time. They wouldn't ask how I was doing (or feeling) but they'd make sure I was still there. Sometimes they'd bring me books they thought I'd like.

One day, one of the ladies asked me to read her the description next to the picture. It's obvious to me now that she suspected I couldn't read and she was probing, but of course I didn't know that at the time.

I told her I couldn't read. She said she would teach me. So every day after school (where they didn't care that I couldn't read) I'd come to the library and learn.

Looking back, it's insane that neither my mother nor anyone at school took an interest in my education. Maybe they thought I was a lost cause and wrote me off. Or maybe it was just a function of school overcrowding. With thirty-five kids to a class how could a teacher pay attention to every student?

I'm lucky I didn't become an adult illiterate. I've met a few. The boyfriend of my sister-in-law is one of them. They gave him a high school diploma even though he couldn't read (or do math). They just passed him from grade to grade and nobody intervened. Finally in his late forties he decided it was time, so he taught himself to read. I'm sure it wasn't easy to learn, and it's not an easy thing to admit. But he did it and now he's a voracious reader.

I hired a retired special ed teacher to tutor my son. She didn't learn to read until she was almost thirty. Eventually she got a PhD. So it can be done. You can learn later. But I'm glad I started when I did.

I knew my alphabet, so that was a good start. The librarian gave me "see spot run" type stuff and taught me phonics. Pretty soon I was on to Dr. Seuss. The rhyming is great for new readers. It's a good way to learn how to sight-read. And I loved Dr. Seuss. I devoured it all.

By the end of the school year I had made good progress and was reading more advanced stuff. She introduced me to *The Boxcar Children* book series by Gertrude Chandler Warner, then I moved on to more mature stuff like *The Hardy Boys* and (yes, I must confess) *Nancy Drew*.

The librarian would also send me home with books. She got me a library card and, after hours, I'd take my books home. Deep into a book, I could sit and escape and be absorbed by the story and disregard the chaos and insanity and sometimes the violence of my home.

It saved me. It absolutely saved me. It gave me something. I'm not sure I would have survived without it.

My kids like to read and they love our town library. We live in a small city outside a large metro area. Somehow the city fathers have kept the library clean. It's not full of homeless, and anybody caught jerking off gets a swift beatdown from the cops at the police station next door.

But we're lucky because most libraries have gone to shit.

I met a friend for lunch recently. We met halfway in the old downtown of what used to be a farming community that's been absorbed into the sprawl. After the lunch, as I was walking back to the car, I felt the urge to pee, so I popped into the public library.

The first thing that hit me was the smell. It was that sour smell of urine-soaked vagrants, but it also smelled like semen. The semen smell got stronger as I walked from the front desk through the stacks to the men's room.

There were no doors on the stalls. Actually there was no door on the men's room. The fluorescent lights had been replaced by black lights and my white shirt glowed. It felt like a '90s rave. The black light makes it harder for junkies to find a vein, thus dissuading them from shooting up (and overdosing) in the library. Now they're all doing fentanyl, which is smoked instead of injected, but the black lights remain.

This was one of those restrooms where it's safer not to wash your hands. My penis was the cleanest/safest thing in this place and that's all I touched during my visit.

It was no place for decent people, and it was certainly no place for children. I would never allow my children to be anywhere near a place like this. But yet they had a children's section. It was next to the men's room. It smelled like cum.

And this was a suburban library in a fairly decent community. Maybe not the nicest town in the metro area, but it's not down-market, and it's certainly not the hood. But sadly, libraries in that dirty (and dangerous) condition are the rule, not the exception.

So why is it even here? Why not close it? Why not tear it down and build a park? Why do we live with this rot and decay?

And if I was growing up today instead of in 1980s America, then where would I go? Who would teach and tutor me? How would I have escaped?

What happens to kids like me? Who saves them?

A FAST-PACED EXCITING ENVIRONMENT

n the pre-smartphone era, I had a producer friend. We weren't super close but he was the boyfriend of my then-girlfriend's best friend. So there were lots of dinners and a couple vacations together. Grownup double-date-type stuff.

This guy was nice enough, but he had his eye on the long game of becoming Above the Line.

("Below the Line" people are the camera guys, assistant directors, lighting guys, and work-a-day producers like me. "Above the Line" people are directors, writers, actors, and producers who get some sort of equity—a percentage of the profits.)

I mostly liked this guy, but the thing that drove me crazy was that he would always answer the phone at inopportune times.

Movies, concerts, dinners, on a tropical beach. He'd always take the call.

One night after he answered his phone in the middle of a crowded movie theater, I straight-up told him, "Bro, you need to turn that thing off."

In his own defense he said, "I have to take every call. Because if I don't take the call they're going to call someone else and that might be a six-figure missed call."

He was right. Those last-minute phone calls placed at 9 p.m., 10 p.m., even after midnight, can be incredibly lucrative. And it's not just about the money. If you miss the call but someone else picks up, they're going to use that person and probably stick with them for a long time. So you lose out on future opportunities as well.

So you gotta take the call. The Business doesn't sleep, and it won't wait for you to get out of the movie theater because:

Things.

Move.

Fast.

Something I see in random job listings: "Fast-paced environment." They don't know what "fast-paced" means. I don't know of another industry that moves with the same intensity as The Business. Maybe stock/commodities trading? An inner-city ER?

My world was nonstop. When I wasn't working I was on call, on standby, because I never knew when the call would come.

I used to keep a suitcase packed at all times. I'd be eating dinner or playing with the kids and the phone would ring and I'd have to rush to the airport to catch a red-eye to god knows where.

It goes without saying that this is not easy on a marriage.

⬛⬛⬛⬛

I was filming in Alberta. Another production was filming a movie with The Rock in the same area where we were shooting, and the cast and crew were staying at our hotel. The place was built for the 1988 Winter Games but it was falling apart—very *Hot Tub Time Machine*.

So I get stuck in the elevator. It was me and the Teamster transportation coordinator from the other movie. The elevator was small, and Teamsters are large men. We got to talking. He had been going from show to show to show for the last three years and hadn't been home in something like eighteen months. His wife filed for divorce that very day. His kids wouldn't talk to him.

You can't say no to a project because, again, they're going to find someone else and stick with that person and then you're sitting at home worrying about money.

And saying "I need to see my wife and kids or my wife is going to leave me" is not an excuse.

He was a nice guy, and I assume he was very good at his job. I'm glad he's keeping busy.

⬛⬛⬛⬛

Once you're in a project, it's nonstop. Every waking hour is calls, emails, decisions. I don't believe that anyone can actually multi-task, but you have to be able to task-switch and stay organized and not forget what you were doing before you switched tasks.

The best system I've found is an old-fashioned notebook with a to-do list. I add and cross things out as needed and try to triage the most important requests. Not high tech, but very effective.

So, you're busy. Crazy busy. And if you're not crazy busy, then people don't want you.

An unwritten rule for Below the Line people like me is to never, *ever* say you're taking time off or going on vacation. You always tell them that you're booked on something else. And if they push about what you're working on, then you lie and make something up.

Never tell them you're taking time for yourself. That might alert them to the fact that you're tired or approaching the dreaded burnout. No one wants someone who's approaching burnout.

As for taking a vacation, it can provoke resentment.

"Oh, I'm stuck here working on this shit show and you're going fishing in the Bahamas? Well fuck you buddy. . . ."

And they want people who are busy. Because like the Teamster in the broken Canadian elevator, it means you're very good at what you do.

I recently heard a great word for pretending to be busier than you really are. It's called *faux-mentum*, as in "fake momentum." It's the perfect way to phrase it.

Always be "in development" or "meeting with" or "optioning" or "negotiating," and never let them know it's actually kind of slow right now but it's nice because I need to catch up on some life stuff and get the car serviced and see a dentist.

Because if you say you're in a slow period they'll say, "Oh good for you! We all need to take a break once in a while," and then they'll never call you again.

This is the root of what I like to call Hollywood Bullshit.

You talk to these people and you never know what's true, what's hyperbolic, or what's outright bullshit. It's a slippery slope from exaggeration and hyperbole to outright lies.

And the system selects for lies.

▪▪▪▪▪

Back when I was a PA, my phone-answering-in-a-movie-theater producer buddy dragged me to a "Film Mixer" networking event. I didn't want to go, but I found out there was free booze and reluctantly went along.

We were poolside at a hotel in Santa Monica and the place was full of guys with shiny open-chest shirts and a bunch of tacky women who looked like they came from extras casting.

I started talking to someone about this movie I had just wrapped and the next one I was about to start. I was telling stories about being a PA (someone who basically gets coffee for people) when I suddenly realized there was a crowd around me.

Everyone was eagerly listening, leaning in, and fake laughing. "OH MY GOD, NO WAY, RRRREALLY?"

I was a PA. I was in jeans and a T-shirt, and they were dressed up. Why were they leaning in? Why were they laughing? What was going on here?

Then I started talking to them. I said, "So what are you up to?" and they fed me some BS like, "Well I think so-and-so really likes my script and we're in talks with such-and-such."

Suddenly it hit me. Not only were all of these people full of shit, but my producer buddy and I were the *only* ones at the event who were actually earning a living in the industry.

I felt ill. What was I doing here, and who were these people, and who was paying for this booze?

▪▪▪▪

I hate lies and I hate liars. From early on in my time in The Business I went out of my way to avoid the scummy types we think of as "Hollywood" people.

I stayed away from the parts of LA where they hung out, and I rarely went to industry parties because they were always there. And it was because of them that I never wanted to climb to Above the Line world. It would mean existing among them, day after day, and having to deal with their constant bullshit.

The world I worked in, which is the world that most industry people are in, is relatively free of bullshit. You do your job, do it well, get paid, go home. It's straightforward.

You're accountable for your work. You either do a good job or you don't. You're easy to work with or you're not.

And the final product is transparent. Everyone sees it. Just like an incompetent carpenter can't hide a house that's off plumb, you can't hide a piece-of-shit movie.

That said, sometimes the movie I worked on *was* a piece of shit, but as long as my work was solid I had no problems. It's not the fault of the carpenter if the architect is bad at his job.)

In what I do now my integrity is very valuable. In fact, it might be my most marketable quality. People take me at my word. If I say a project is possible, then they believe me, and I pull it off.

The flip side is that sometimes people come to me with projects that are not possible to pull off.

What I could do is bullshit them and say, "It's a great idea, guys, no problem, this is going to be easy," and then collect the paycheck while the whole thing falls apart.

But I don't do that. I give them my honest assessment even if it means losing the job.

There's a short-term financial penalty, but it pays in the long run. If I have any equity at all in the industry it's wrapped up in my integrity. So bullshit just isn't going to pay long-term.

But sometimes I think, What if?

What if I would have agreed to the bullshit and gone to all those (incredibly boring) parties and fake laughed at everyone's stories and kept up the faux-mentum? Could I have made it to the top?

Maybe.

But at what cost? What would I have become? What would I have lost along the way?

My honest assessment is that I could not have lived with myself. I would have become just like them, and it would have eaten away at me. The cracks in my soul would have grown. And quite frankly, it's nice to be able to look myself in the eye when I brush my teeth.

THE GATOR

heard a story. You could almost call this a Production Urban Legend. It's one of those stories that goes around and gets better with each new retelling.

Here's the version I heard:

It was a shoot in Mexico. They were doing a scene in a shack in some favela. It was a mixed crew. The principal actors and key crew were American, the rest of the crew were Mexicans.

So they were shooting in this shack doing some heavy dialog scene, but there was a dog barking somewhere in the neighborhood. It was ruining the sound and they kept blowing takes. Finally, the American 1st AD got on the walkie and asked for someone to stop the dog from barking.

But the dog didn't stop. He kept on barking and takes kept getting blown.

The AD lost it. He marched out of the shack and started shouting, "Somebody kill the dog! Kill the fucking dog right now!"

In industry jargon, to "kill" something means to "please make that stop," as in "kill the lights" or "kill the smoke." But a Mexican PA, who was very dedicated to his job and spoke English as a second language, took the order literally. He found the dog and . . . killed it.

The crew was horrified, but the problem was solved. The PA got an order and made it happen. Now that's a good PA.

I'm sure he had a bright future in the Mexican film industry. But then again, maybe not. Most likely nobody remembered him. His heroism in the line of duty was probably ignored. Because taking extreme measures to "make things happen" is not always rewarded. Sometimes it's even punished.

That story gets repeated as a cautionary tale of taking the job too seriously. "Don't be the PA who killed the dog." In other words, use your head before following through with a crazy request.

But the story also speaks to a larger dilemma. In The Business, there's often a fine line between doing what's expected, and doing something that's dangerous or criminal or just plain stupid.

The mantra you hear over and over is that you're only as good as your last job. From your first days on a set, you learn that you gotta do whatever it takes. You have to get the job done. No matter what, you have to "make it happen."

Because if you don't, you'll be replaced. And make no mistake: There's a long line of people waiting for your job.

As an AD friend likes to say, "There are vending machines full of guys like you."

At the same time, The Business does not tolerate mistakes or fuckups. It does not abide caution or ethical scruples. And it most certainly does not care if you're feeling overwhelmed by pressure or are concerned that you might not be able to "get it done."

And so sometimes you find yourself doing things you would not ordinarily do—like killing an innocent animal or, say, committing a felony.

So here's another story. This one happened to me. The statute of limitations has expired so I think it's safe to tell the tale.

This is what happened:

I was a PA on a shoot in San Francisco. It was a Sunday evening. The next morning we were doing a dawn shot on the Embarcadero.

The director had (what she thought was) an innocuous request. She wanted to put the Steadicam operator in a golf cart to track our actors as they walked down the sidewalk next to the bay. "No problem," the production manager said. "We'll make it happen."

In LA, procuring a golf cart on a Sunday night is a simple task. Hollywood runs 24/7 and the vendors who service The Business specialize in accommodating last-minute requests.

Need a specialty piece of equipment on the weekend? No problem! There might be an additional fee to open the shop and deliver the equipment, but it's never an issue because everyone lives by the mantra of "make it happen."

But we weren't shooting in LA. We were shooting in San Francisco. And the people who live in San Francisco believe "quality of life" is more important than "make it happen" and don't pick up the phone at 5 p.m. on a Sunday afternoon.

After making some calls and finding that everyone was closed, the production team started to panic. The director had made a request and that request must be filled no matter what. The repercussions ranged from outright firing to long-term career damage. At a minimum, they would never work for that director again.

And no, you can't negotiate the request. There are many instances in the Bible of people negotiating with God (the Sodom and Gomorrah story comes to mind), but there's no way a production team can negotiate with a director. It just doesn't happen. The production team is there to follow orders, to "get the job done." Saying no isn't an option.

So for us it meant we couldn't ask to push the shot to later in the day, after the vendors were open, or could we do it on Tuesday, or could we just kill this thing all together and stick with the original plan without the golf cart?

No. The request had to be honored. We had to cater to this whim.

After running out of proper golf cart rental vendors to contact, the production team and I frantically started calling every crew member asking if they happened to know where we could get a golf cart.

At this point it was 10 p.m. and we were striking out. Until . . . we reached one of the art assistants.

It turned out he had just wrapped another shoot that very day. They'd been working at Ocean Beach and had used a number of Gators. The Gators were still sitting in the beach parking lot waiting to be picked up the next day.

A John Deere Gator is a gas-powered side-by-side utility vehicle with a top speed of about 20 mph. Think all-terrain golf cart. We commonly use Gators to move equipment to hard-to-reach places where our rolling carts can't go—like beaches. It wasn't *exactly* a golf cart, but we could make it work for the tracking shot.

Problem solved, right?

Wrong.

It wasn't solved because we needed to get the Gator from the beach to the bayside of San Francisco in time for a 5 a.m. dawn shot.

But the production manager had a solution: She told me that I was to go to the beach, steal a Gator, and drive it to the Embarcadero—on the other side of San Francisco.

I balked. No fucking way was I doing that.

How was I supposed to drive an off-road vehicle across the entirety of the San Francisco Peninsula without getting pulled over? Would I spend the night in jail? Or longer?

The production manager pleaded with me. She said there was no one else to do it (this was true) and that she'd smooth things over with the Gator rental company and the cops if I got caught.

Still I refused. Though I knew little about the law, I did know quite a bit about the criminal class of San Francisco. I certainly did not want to be locked in the SF County Jail with the most disgusting degenerates in the Western world.

The production manager was not happy. Her pleading turned to threats. She threatened me not only with getting fired from this production (which, by that point, I couldn't have cared less), but said she would blackball me with other producers and production managers and anyone else who would listen.

This was the "you'll never work in this town again" threat. Now things were getting serious. It was (and still is) possible to blackball someone. The production manager could very easily spread poisonous rumors to other producers about my character and willingness to "get the job done," and there unquestionably would be consequences.

And so, under duress, I agreed to the Great San Francisco Gator Caper.

I got to the beach around midnight. The Gators were parked where the art assistant said they would be. There were no cops or security. Nobody in sight. Just me, the cold ocean air, and the barking of sea lions.

This was going to be the perfect crime, I thought. I would just drive the thing across town, the production manager would call the rental company in the morning to smooth things out, and I would be the hero. What could possibly go wrong?

But things didn't go quite as planned.

The first thing that went wrong was I couldn't find a key. They're usually hidden somewhere on the vehicle. I checked the glove box, under the seats, on top of the tires, and under the hood in the air filter box. No keys.

So I went to Plan B. I got a flathead screwdriver from my truck. Then I found a nice grapefruit-sized rock at the edge of the parking lot. I jammed the flathead into the ignition, then pounded it with the rock until I cracked the lock cylinder. After that I was able to start the engine with a turn of the screwdriver.

San Francisco is famously seven miles square. Seven by seven as they say. I was at mile zero and my destination was seven miles east (more or less).

I left the beach lot and drove into Golden Gate Park.

This was the easy part of the journey. Driving the Gator I looked like a park department maintenance guy. At night the park is full of meth addicts and cruising gays, but they tend to stay out of sight. In fact I didn't see anybody. It probably helped that I stayed off the roads and stuck to the paths and sidewalks.

The white-knuckling really started when I got to the eastern edge of the park at Stanyan. I could have kept going straight through the middle of the Golden Gate Park Panhandle, but it parallels Fell and Oak streets—major thoroughfares—and I didn't want to risk running into SF's finest.

So I zigzagged in a northeastern direction, through the Western Addition, across Geary Boulevard, then through Japantown. I blew through all the lights and stop signs because, well, I'm already committing a felony so fuck it—I might as well tack on some moving violations.

The Gator, as an off-road vehicle, had headlights but no brake- or tail-lights. It was also loud—like a motorcycle but with a more annoying, grating sound. At one point I looked behind me and saw a string of lights being turned on as I woke up the neighborhood.

Lucky for me SFPD doesn't respond to noise complaints.

Eventually I made it across Van Ness, then up Nob Hill. I briefly considered taking the notoriously twisty Lombard Street, but that was just asking for trouble. I could have lost it on a curve, and since the street passed through an expensive neighborhood and was a popular spot for guys to race tuned-up rice-rockets, there was usually a cop nearby.

Instead, I did more zigzagging through Chinatown, ignoring the pungent smell of Chinese restaurant garbage. Finally I drove full tilt through the Financial District on the way to the Embarcadero.

I left the Gator with a security guard who was making sure no one stole our posted parking.

After showing him how to use the screwdriver key (in case someone needed to move the Gator before I returned), I walked to the North Beach red-light district to flag a taxi back to the ocean. I retrieved my truck, drove back to my hotel, and crashed out. It was about 3 a.m. I had to be on set in two hours.

I mentioned above that the first thing to go wrong with the caper was not being able to find the key. The next thing that went wrong was that I got fired.

I didn't get caught jacking the Gator, and thankfully I did not spend the night in the county jail with a crew of shit-stained crackheads. But yes, I did get fired.

I was late to set due to my after-hours criminality. Also, the producer did not like my "attitude." Or at least that's what I heard—the producer didn't have the stones to fire me in person, so she had the production coordinator do it instead.

As she was firing me on the street in front of the production trailer, I eyeballed a group of SFPD officers that we had hired to help with traffic control. They were gathered around the Gator looking at the screwdriver jammed in the ignition.

I never worked with that team again, but I don't think they went out of their way to blackball me.

Oh, and after all that—after all the stress and criminality—they never even used the Gator.

Sometime in the night, after I had liberated the Gator and was racing through the streets of SF, stressing over cops and my future in The Business, the director decided to change the shot. These creatives can be fickle and that's just how it goes. However, I don't think the director had any idea what I went through fulfilling her seemingly simple request.

But I made it happen, dammit. I pulled it off.

Like a good little soldier, I "got the job done."

And no animals were harmed.

FAMILY

was talking to a friend. Relating the story of how my cousin wasn't at a recent family gathering because he was on the run from the law.

He had a drug lab in his house. It got raided. He jumped bail in May and was still running. Nobody knew where he was. His stepmom said he wasn't going to surrender, that he would go down fighting.

I'm five years older than he is. It was a big difference when we were kids, but now we're contemporaries. Contemporaries, except he's always been a mess. His mom died when he was young, about ten years old. It traumatized him. He became a juvenile delinquent.

My dad died when I was about my cousin's age. Dad had been sick. I went to see *Teenage Mutant Ninja Turtles*. I took the bus with friends. You could do that then.

I got home and Mom sat me down. She told me that my dad had died.

I turned into a juvenile delinquent too. Lots of drugs early. Dropped out of high school. Never got arrested though. I could always talk my way out of it.

My cousin wasn't as bright as me. He wasn't able to talk his way out of an arrest.

One night, drunk and high and armed with a lifted piece-of-shit truck, he decided to start driving through suburban backyards. Just smashing through the fences at high speed, crushing flowerbeds and patio furniture.

This was before smartphones and home security cams so there's no video. But I'd like to imagine his truck covered in hammocks and fencing and flowers as he's killdozering through the suburbs.

He made it through a few blocks of yards before he drove into a pool. The SWAT team had been deployed by this point. This is in the interior of America and people have guns. The neighbors were about to lynch him when the cops got him.

But he was still a minor so he got a relatively light slap. He had to go to juvie, but they let him out on his eighteenth birthday with an expunged record. There was also a *giant* lawsuit, but that's another story. . . .

Later there was another incident where he rode his dirt bike off a cliff. He was high on meth. Said he missed the turn in the trail but I'm not so sure. He was going full throttle—literally and figuratively—and he didn't care if he lived or died. 2 high 2 die.

Somehow he survived. They had to life flight him out. It was a long recovery. He broke just about everything. But it woke him up and he mellowed out—for a few years anyway.

We lost touch along the way. I got busy with life and had no time for my junkie cousin. I was actually shocked to hear that he was still alive. He was allegedly manufacturing "bath salts" (a synthetic cocaine-type drug) in his house.

His stepmom told me the story about the drug raid and how he jumped bail while I was at the family gathering. She was hurting; his dad (my uncle) couldn't even talk about it. I didn't know what to say and mumbled something about how sorry I was and how they should hire a good lawyer.

His stepmom said, "He's not going to surrender."

I was stunned. "So he's . . . going to go down fighting?"

She nodded silently. I didn't know what to say. There was nothing I could say.

Anyway, I was telling this story to a friend. And she asked, "Why doesn't he get his shit together?"

So I said, "Well his mom died when he was young, and dad was a Nam vet and got really fucked up over there and—"

She cut me off.

My friend said she thinks Vietnam introduced multigenerational trauma (aka intergenerational trauma) the likes of which we've never seen. Talked about her ex-boyfriend. Dad was a Nam vet, and the kids are all fucked up. She said it poisoned our entire society.

So I thought about my uncle and my cousin and his family, and I couldn't help but think that she wasn't wrong.

∎∎∎∎

Intergenerational trauma. I hate that phrase. It's such a woke shitlib thing to say. And it *is* a shitlib way to think: that someone (or a large group of somebodies) cannot help but be shitty fucked-up criminals because something horrifically bad happened in the past.

And it's funny how it's the exception to the liberal idea of blank slatism. You're born a completely blank slate and only susceptible to environmental factors, unless your ancestor went through some shit. And then you just can't help yourself because intergenerational trauma. Got it.

My wife and I made friends with another couple when we escaped California for the middle of America. They became dear friends. Our kids went to school with their kids. This is how friends are made when you're a married adult with children.

They were wonderful people. Very Christian. They were pastors. They did Christian therapy. They wanted to help people heal their trauma and find Jesus. Noble work really.

And then during the Great Sorting of 2020 and the Summer of Floyd something changed. They left their church. Questioned their faith. They went woke.

Suddenly they had one of those "In This House We Believe" signs in their yard. There was a Black Lives Matter sign in their living room.

The BLM thing offended me. Because I knew BLM hates Jews. And I knew BLM isn't friend to me or my half-Jewish children.

We drifted apart. I couldn't hold a conversation with them. Because we were no longer having the same conversation. Their minds had been infected. I couldn't be around them any longer, and they didn't want to be around me. The backyard barbecue invites stopped coming. I wasn't welcome.

But my wife was friends with the wife and my oldest son was (and is) best buddies with their oldest son, so I'd still see them. It was usually in passing when I was picking up my son from a birthday party or sleepover.

The wife was going back to school for a master's or doctorate and she was doing her thesis on intergenerational trauma. She was interested in the Jewish American experience and how the trauma my ancestors went through may have affected me. She wanted to do an interview.

But we never did the interview. She never followed up. I suspect my wife related stories about my family and my childhood and she probably thought it was so fucked up that she dropped the issue.

Or maybe she thought it wouldn't have looked good to her woke faculty advisors to delve too deeply into the life of a White Mostly-Jewish Man.

And while it sounds absurd, just because shitlibs talk about multigenerational trauma doesn't mean that it's not a thing. That it's not real. It *is* real. I've felt it.

I for one firmly believe that I'm a product of my ancestors. I'd like to think that I'm a product of their success, genetic and otherwise. Because if they hadn't succeeded then I wouldn't be here, right?

But it's far far more complicated than that. And I'm not just a product of their genetics or their successes or their failures. I carry other things with me too.

▪▪▪▪

In Hollywood, careers are often built on nepotism. But not in my case. In fact, in my case it actually hurt me.

There's a city on the California coast. I don't want to get too specific but it's between LA and San Francisco. I'm not allowed to film in this city. And the reason I'm not allowed to film in this city started about a decade before I was even born.

Here's the story:

There was a rock band. They were special. They were "discovered" by this young Jewish woman who was the booker at a Hollywood music venue. They were going to be the Next Big Thing. She was in love with the singer and she was going to manage the band and ride that thang all the way to the top. The big record labels were circling. She must have been thrilled.

But . . . the father of one of the guys in the band had done business with my dad and knew he worked in the music biz (all over show biz actually), so the band hired my dad to represent them.

The first thing my dad did was kick that bitch who worked at the club. Kicked her to the curb.

The second thing he did was get the band a great record deal. Then he got them competent management and made sure they were set for life. And they *were* set for life, even though not all of them lived that long (it was the '60s, man).

So the booker ended up marrying some guy, and, as aging hippies do, they left the big city to live a quiet life on the Central Coast. Eventually she became the local film commissioner.

And then, forty years after my dad met the band, I tried to produce a shoot in her town. She found out I was my father's son and seemed thrilled to hear this. We had a cordial chat, with her sharing memories about my dad and also asking me about my life.

It was a great conversation. I rarely get to talk to people who knew my father. Most of his contemporaries were long gone by the time I reached adulthood. So to find a link to his past was wonderful. It's a link to my past, a link to where I came from.

And then she knifed me in the back.

The night before the shoot she canceled the permits and pulled the locations. I was fucked. Payback from the late '60s for shit that happened ten years before I was born.

Amazing.

I knew it was payback because she told me it was payback. Actually, "told" isn't quite the right word—she screamed it at me over the phone. Said, "People like you LIE AND LIE AND LIE AND THEN PEOPLE END UP DEAD!" Thus blaming me for the drug-related death of her rockstar ex-boyfriend that happened before my parents even met.

My career took a giant fucking hit from this, by the way. How big a hit, I don't know for sure. But it set me back a few years.

I had even explained to this woman that I never really knew my father. My parents divorced when I was two. We moved to another state. Then he died when I was twelve. And I told her (quite sincerely) that it was nice to make a connection with someone who knew him.

A few things still amaze and puzzle me about this incident. One is how someone could hold onto that much hatred and resentment for thirty-plus years. (Because hell hath no fury like a woman scorned. That's why.)

The other thing that amazes me is how one of my father's many successful business deals could come back and bite me in the ass. Was this some sort of karma?

And then I wonder, What things have I done that will come back to bite my kids in the ass? Or what things WILL I do?

My dad was just doing his job. He was doing the best he could for his clients. I'm sure he saw that woman and said, "No, not her." And he was right. A spiteful jealous woman would have dragged that band down.

My dad's dad had been some sort of gangster in the Old Country. One of my uncles (who died long before I was born) wrote a great memoir.

My uncle's earliest memory concerned a hitman. A rival gangster had hired a Turkish hitman from Odessa to kill his father (my grandfather). The hitman came at my grandfather with a scythe, Grim Reaper style. He swung and missed and then got tackled and beaten *to death* by a bunch of angry Jews. (Life in the shtetl was rough, man.)

In the 1960s my dad was older than I am now. He'd seen stuff. Done stuff. He had life wisdom and he saw that woman and knew she was trouble. So he kicked her. Good work Dad!

Of course he had no idea that he would have another son by another wife and forty years later that son would be a producer trying to produce some shit on the Central Coast and that bitch from the Sunset Strip would still be around and waiting for her revenge.

▪▪▪▪▪

My dad was World War II generation. He had me late in life. His dad had him late in life, so his dad (my grandfather) was a veteran of the Russo-Japanese War.

After one particularly horrific pogrom he took his family to the USA where my father was born. They settled in the Southern Plains, started a cattle ranch. His brother did the same thing in Argentina.

Grandfather (let's call him Hershel Van Halen) was denied land, horses, and guns in the Old Country and that's all he wanted in the New Country.

And he got it. All of it. Lots of it. They thrived.

A family story is that there was oil on the land. A lot of oil. But Hershel didn't want to develop the oil because he thought it would be bad for the cattle.

Quick aside: I heard this story about the oil and cattle when I was a kid and thought, Haha funny story. Then I saw the movie *Giant* (1956) and there's a very similar oil/cow story that's essential to the plot. I'd say that someone in my family stole the story about the oil and the cattle from *Giant*. However, I later learned that my father knew Edna Ferber, who wrote the novel that *Giant* is based on. So did she hear the oil/cow story from my dad?

Anyway, things were going great for Hershel and the Van Halens, then the Depression hit and he lost just about everything. The stress of it ended up killing him.

The kids sold the land (which may or may not have had oil) and did quite well. My father, the baby of the family, was the only one who worked. His older brothers decided to retire to California and my dad went with them.

My dad got out of law school right as the war was ending. He was in the right place at the right time. The studio system was breaking up and suddenly actors needed representation.

He was a socialite and knew lots of celebrities and suddenly he became one of the first entertainment lawyers. It was a completely new legal discipline, and he basically wrote the book on it.

I'd love to tell you more of his story but it would undoubtedly get me doxxed.

But here's a key point: he had weaknesses.

One was gambling. My mother told me a story. He lost $750,000 in 1975 dollars at a Vegas craps table in one night.

For visits he used to fly in and pick me up so I wouldn't have to fly alone (that was nice actually). One time LAX was fogged in and we were diverted to Vegas. Caesars Palace found out he was landing and sent a limo. They comped us a suite. It was the suite from *Rain Man*.

His other weakness was women. Even to the end of his life (and he died an old man) there was gambling and there were women.

They were hot women too. Always. Women loved him. I don't know how he did it. It's always puzzled me.

As an adult man of the world I've been around men with trophy wives or straight-up hookers on their arms. These women have nothing but contempt for Sugar Daddy. They resent being kept. They resent being dependent. The resentment turns to hatred. And Sugar Daddy knows this, but it's all part of the game. It's all part of what it's like to be him, owning the yacht and the supercar and the beachfront house, and keeping beautiful women. It's another thing he possesses to show he's not a fraud and that he's worth what he's worth.

But it wasn't like that with my dad. These women loved him. Genuinely loved him. And I think, in a way, he loved them back.

My mom was an actress. She had some success on Broadway, and like so many beautiful women she moved out to LA to parlay her looks and her talent into Hollywood stardom. But just like for most women, it didn't work out. She had a recurring role on a soap opera but never made it into movies.

Then she met my dad. She had a child (me), and that's the end of anyone's acting career. She wasn't content to be a side piece and she made him marry her. He wasn't content to have a gentile wife so she converted to Judaism. He still had to divorce his first wife, and that took some time, but he made it happen.

The marriage didn't last. Though there was a thirty-year age gap, he started sleeping with even younger women. Mom wouldn't suffer through that and she left. We moved to another state where she could ski and be closer to her family.

Dad started dating a twenty-year-old model. He would have been about seventy at this point.

Actually, she was nineteen, but twenty doesn't sound as gross so let's go with that.

Dad ended up marrying her. I heard she got him drunk in Vegas and coerced him into it, but I'm not so sure. He probably went willingly. Because she was hot. So fucking hot.

I vividly remember my first erection. I was in LA on a visit. Stepmom was walking around the house naked. I got rock hard. It was painful. I didn't know what it was. It was terrifying.

She came to check to see why I was in pain, saw my boner, then rushed to put some clothes on. I would have been about five.

■■■■■

One day, after many years of bad marriage, and a few weeks after his cancer diagnosis, my dad comes home and finds the locks have been changed. The little Gold Digger had decided to start digging for the gold. . . .

This was his third divorce and he decided she wasn't going to get a penny. He came up with a two-part plan.

First, he dragged the divorce out up to his death.

Second, he set out to blow his entire fortune so she wouldn't get a dime.

He spent most of the rest of his life (about three years) living in hotels in Beverly Hills and Newport Beach. By the very end, when he could no longer take care of himself, he moved in with an old girlfriend in Westwood.

He was still married to my stepmom when he died. He was also broke. Mission accomplished. He went out in style, I'll give him that.

Except . . . he left me virtually nothing.

My mom was terrible with money. She lost most of her divorce settlement through bad real estate investments. And she couldn't properly budget what income she had coming in. She was always spending money on stupid things. We got by on food stamps and government cheese (it was the '80s), though sometimes we had no food at all.

I hated birthdays. I still dread them. My mother (God bless her) would blow a bunch of money on an expensive gift or outing to make my birthday "special." But then we wouldn't have money to buy food for a month.

Now, when my wife asks me what I want for my birthday, I just ask to go out for a nice dinner. I can't stand getting presents. If you're going to buy me a present, please buy food. Food insecurity (the new euphemism for "hunger") isn't something you ever get over.

Actresses can starve themselves, but growing kids can't.

I'd be remiss if I didn't mention that in many ways my mother was an amazing woman. She somehow put herself through law school as a single mom with three kids. Eventually she attained financial security, but it wasn't until I was a teenager and already out of the house.

But as a child I was adept at eating dinner at friends' homes and scrounging under vending machines. People were always dropping coins under vending machines at the neighborhood hospital, and the arms of a child were small enough to retrieve them. If I could find fifty cents, I could buy school lunch.

My stepmom, the nineteen-year-old model, had a serious coke problem. But even worse, she was addicted to the Beverly Hills Trophy-Wife Lifestyle. The death of my father left her without income. So, utilizing her assets (her hotness), she went to work as an escort for a notorious Madame to the Stars.

That is, until the madame got busted. It was all over the news about the "Madam to the Stars" and which celebs could possibly be in her Little Black Book.

One of the names in the book was my gold-digging whore step-mother. And her name got published.

I forget which show it was, but one of the tabloid TV shows did an ambush interview with her on the street in Beverly Hills.

It aired and then she killed herself. I think it was the next day. It was an overdose, but one of my older half-brothers is convinced it was murder—that someone gave her a hot dose.

I was in junior high when this happened. Before her death she would call our house in the middle of the night. She would ask for me, and I have no idea why, but my mom would let her talk to me.

She would be all coked out and ask me to help her find the money my dad had "hidden" in Swiss banks. There were millions, she said. But there was no money, and that bitch was crazy.

I remember she wouldn't let my dad into their house to get his stuff, including his suits. So my dad got a court order.

When stepmom finally complied and sent over the suits, he found she had taken little scissors (probably cuticle scissors) and cut thousands of little holes into each suit. It must have taken her days of cutting.

It was the only time I saw my dad cry.

She must have been amazing in bed though. Hot + crazy is a winning combo for the horny man. Until she ruins your life, that is.

Pussy is one hell of a drug.

░░░░

Cut to 1995 and I'm in a movie theater watching Martin Scorsese's *Casino*. And it was her. Sharon Stone was *her*. She *was* my stepmother. Same clothes, same car, same coke problem, same mannerisms, same voice.

Sharon plays a blonde in the film and my stepmom had jet black hair, but other than that she was *the same*. She even died in the same way—with the De Niro character speculating about the hot dose.

I left the theater pale and shaking. My date was asking me if I was okay. I'd seen a ghost. It was *her*.

My stepmom and Sharon Stone were about the same age, and I'm pretty sure they ran in the same circles in the '80s. I can't say for certain, but it's possible they may even have been friends.

But *were* they friends? Was Sharon Stone's character in *Casino* some sort of tribute to my stepmother? If I ever meet Sharon, I'll be sure to ask.

▪▪▪▪▪

I have so many unanswered questions. And most of them will probably remain unanswered, because the people with the answers are dead.

For example, after my mom died I opened her safe deposit box and found (among other things) a stack of Krugerrands and a bag of uncut diamonds.

We were on food stamps when I was a kid. So where did this come from?

I also found old passports. I admired her passport pictures. She was beautiful. It was a much younger mom. The Broadway actress mom. My mother before she became a mother. Truly beautiful. Even on her deathbed she was still beautiful.

But then I started flipping through the pages in those old passports issued before I was born. The stamps were from all over. Iran, Saudi Arabia, Yugoslavia, Czech Republic, Hong Kong, Yemen.

Yemen? Who went to Yemen in the 1970s? Who went to any of these places in the 1970s? Why would a beautiful blonde American actress go there?

This was the passport of an arms dealer. Why did my mom have it?

And you know what . . . I'll never know the answer.

She also left behind some scrapbooks. A lot of publicity photos from her Broadway shows, polaroids, playbills, stuff like that. On one page there was a letter from a producer at *The Dating Game* (no, not Chuck Barris). It expressed polite displeasure that she'd backed out of a taping, but wished her well in her future endeavors, etc. Why did she keep this? To remind herself of the time she wasn't on *The Dating Game*? More unanswered questions.

She told me one story about her time in New York. When she first moved there her agent got her a series of gigs as a Beard. She would pretend to "date" gay celebrities so they could be seen in public (and the press) with a hot blonde on their arm. She'd go to dinners, events, and awards shows, and they'd pose for the photographers. Then her "date" would slip into the men's room and hook up with some guy.

Her first beard gig was with a famous classical pianist (not Liberace, but she knew him). She thought it was a real date. Then he disappeared with some guy. The next day she was deeply confused. Her agent had to explain things.

She became close with a lot of those guys. I remember they'd stop in and say hi when they were doing some concert or movie in our part of the country. Very nice guys. But she never left me alone with them.

She did have an affair with a famous singer. I mean, he was *famous*. Big time famous. Larger than life. They went on a date when she was in high school. He was a perfect gentleman and nothing happened.

Cut to 1970-something. She was the lead in a Broadway revival. He came backstage to say hello ("Hey, remember me?"). And then it was on for three or four years. As it turned out, he was married, but when you're famous they let you do these things. . . .

She never told me this story, but I heard it from my sister after she died. I would have had so many questions for her had I known. But now I'll never get the answers.

A big question I have is if the man who I believe to be my father is really my father. Or am I the son of Larger-Than-Life Singer? And is there a way to claim part of that singer's estate?

It would be nice to know.

Nice to know about being an heir to his estate, that is. I'm happy to stay in blissful ignorance about who my actual biological father is. It's part of the reason I've never done a genetic test.

As I've said, I never really knew my dad. That is, my legal dad. The man I called father. I visited him every other weekend, but I was young and I never knew him. Never *really* knew him.

And I never really knew my mom either. Who were these people who made me and raised me?

Recently I asked my sister to tell me the story about Mom and the singer again. It was exactly as I remembered. Except, the part about the affair was gone. She omitted it. She said it never happened. That they were just friends.

But Mom was beautiful, so beautiful. He couldn't have resisted her.

And he was famous, at the peak of his fame, and handsome, and rich. How could she have resisted *him*? Women threw themselves at him. This is a fact. We know this.

But my sister insists: it never happened.

My mom was dying, in hospice, when she told the story to my sister. And my sister and I were drinking when she first told the story to me. Did I not hear her correctly? Did I fill in the blanks with what time has taught me about human nature and men and women?

Or perhaps she changed the story because it's uncomfortable thinking about Mom banging a rock star? And does this mean I don't have to worry about my dad not being my real dad?

All the involved parties are dead. I'll never get the answers.

I won't get answers to most of my questions.

But I do know the answer to some things. Time and wisdom and life have shown me. Like about why my mother was attracted to abusive men, and why she stayed with them even after they hit her. Now I know why.

And if you don't know the answer, you'll learn these things eventually. Life will teach you.

Life teaches you how to live it, if you live long enough.

Tony Bennett said that.

DAIRY QUEEN

I could feel his pain. I could. But I wasn't sure what to do about it.

He came home from school. It was the second week of junior high. He was crying.

I asked him what was wrong. He wouldn't tell me. Asked if we could drive somewhere. So we got in the truck and went.

He told me he liked my new truck. I told him I liked it too.

He was riding up front. Per state safety "recommendations" he should have been in the backseat, but he was up front like a big boy. I still didn't know where we were going.

I suggested ice cream. It was either that or the hardware store—the one with the gun section.

He said ice cream. I offered up the fancy ice cream shop. The one with the crazy flavors all made from organic milk and the machine that makes fresh waffle cones on demand.

He wanted Dairy Queen.

I was good with that. I love Dairy Queen.

Teenagers don't hang out at DQ anymore. They don't work there either.

It was after school and a hot day. It should have been packed with teens. It would have been packed with teens in the '90s. Now it was void of customers. Now grown Latina women worked there. Women with kids. They were blasting that horrid Mexican polka music in the kitchen.

He got chocolate-dipped vanilla. I got regular vanilla. We went outside with our cones.

"So what happened today?"

"Nothing."

"Well, it sounds like something happened buddy." I was using my best matter-of-fact dad voice.

"It was just . . . hard."

A bus rolled up. There's a bus stop in front of the DQ. It came all the way from the Big City, about an hour down the road.

It dropped off the trash then rolled on. But the derelicts just milled about. They didn't have anywhere to go. They went to the Big City to buy drugs. Now they had their drugs and were high. But it wasn't a happy high. Their eyes were dead. They were twitching. Bubbling and popping. Wearing backpacks full of god knows what. Now they were back home, within walking distance of their Section 8 housing.

The city keeps adding more Section 8 housing. And they keep adding buses so the Section 8 residents can go to the Big City and buy drugs. Our city is small and they don't have the resources to fight this.

I instinctively touched my gun just to make sure it was there. I just barely brushed it. I knew it was there but I was compelled to check. It was still there under my T-shirt. Then I shifted on the bench so my back was to the wall and I was facing the bus riders. I wanted a better view of them, but more importantly I wanted them to have a better view of me. I wanted to let them know there was a man here, and I was staking my ground. This bench, this picnic table, this Dairy Queen, this child—they were all mine. My body language said, "This is my space."

When was the last time I cleaned this gun? When was the last time I rotated the ammo? I had a kid to protect and you have to think about these things.

I carry all the time. Even when I'm not around the kids. My new job, the crew work I do since I gave up producing, gets a little sketchy sometimes. I'm out in the field at odd times of day. Sometimes I'm in bad neighborhoods in the city. And there are no good rural areas left. Meth and fentanyl are abundant once you get outside the city. Often I run into sketchy characters. A middle-age ex-producer with a professional camera really sets off the meth-head paranoia. I've had my hand on the gun a few times, but thankfully I've never had to use it.

Though I don't carry to protect myself. I do it so I can make it home to protect the kids. Because in this world, young men need protection. They need fathers.

As I've said, my father wasn't around. I'd visit him quite a bit, but he wasn't there for the day-to-day stuff. My father died when I was about my younger son's age. The son who was sitting in front of me eating soft serve. I think about this quite a bit and I fear leaving my sons like my father left me.

"How was it hard?" I said.

He tried to speak but he couldn't articulate. The most he could get out was "It's like . . .," and then he stopped. He didn't have the language for this.

It took a while, but I got the story. He was having trouble with his teachers. The female teachers.

One of them taught his digital art class. My kid is a good artist. Both of my sons are good artists. They taught themselves to draw in perspective by second grade. My younger son, the one eating ice cream, has a sketchbook full of characters he's designed.

I gave him both volumes of Walt Stanchfield's *Drawn to Life*. Stanchfield was a legendary Disney animator. He'd give lectures to the junior animators about character design, movement, etc. Eventually his lecture notes were compiled into a two-volume set. It's the bible of animation.

My son ate it up.

I also gave him Scott McCloud's *Understanding Comics*. Ostensibly about comic-book theory, it's a wonderful primer for any type of visual media. Both kids love that book.

My son is writing a comic book about a raccoon private detective he calls Trash Panda.

It's cute. Full of kid humor.

But in this "art" class he was given a specific thing to create—that day it was a cat. He was supposed to create an exact copy of the example presented by the teacher. But he decided that was pointless stupid and a little too easy, so he freelanced and did his own thing. Knowing him he probably drew it in perspective. Then he gave it personality. Just like a golden-age Disney animator would give it personality.

I never saw the drawing, but I assume it was good because his other art is good. And because he was trying to impress his teacher and the class I'm sure he made it extra good.

I'm sure he was expecting praise for a job well done. But instead of praise he was yelled at in front of the class.

He said she yelled. I believed my son. He's not a bullshitter. He's not a liar.

I also believed him because, as I've learned myself, there is a certain type of woman who won't hesitate to yell at a young man. And not just in school.

It's happened to me many times. It happened when I was a child. It happened when I was an adult. It happened in professional settings. Once it happened when I was minding my own damn business in a grocery store.

This is something I used to ponder. What would make a woman do this?

I could talk about the reasons—lord knows I could talk about the reasons. From the Jungian Devouring Mother, to creeping socialism, to the insecurity of being a woman surrounded by competent capable men, which breeds hatred and resentment, and on and on.

But in the end I've just accepted that there are simply women who hate men. It's just a fact. There's nothing I can do about this, and the specific reasons for their hatred don't matter. They don't matter because I try not to worry about things I can't control.

Yet I have to send my sons out into a world that's full of hateful resentful women. They'll take out their hatred and aggression and resentment when my sons are at their weakest, when they're at their most vulnerable. That's what these types do. That's how they operate.

But I don't like to think about that. I'd rather think about my sons going out into the world and meeting wonderful women. Because there are wonderful women in this world.

And I mean that in a very literal sense: there are women who are full of wonder. Not just pleasant women, or attractive women, or even sexy women. I'm talking about women who are magical. Women who can intuit things that I can't. Women who *know* things. These are the women who give birth to the world. Like my wife. Like many others.

I think about the women who mentored me in The Business.

I think about one in particular. She won a Golden Globe a few years back. She'd made so many great movies, and she'd received Oscar nominations. But every year she got shafted. These award shows are very political. My mentor and the studio she worked for never had the juice to pull off a win.

But she won the Globe. I got a text from a mutual friend telling me she'd won. I found the clip on the internet. There she was looking shocked, and looking beautiful. She looked truly radiant. It made me happy.

I was so happy I cried. I was sitting in my car watching the video on my phone and crying.

I cried tears of love and gratitude.

She taught me so much, but I don't think it was intentional. We talked recently and I thanked her for her mentorship. I told her that the things she taught me have allowed me to support my family, and to get what I wanted out of The Business so I could do the type of work I was made to do and do it on my own terms in a part of the country that I wanted to live.

I expressed my sincere gratitude. To my shock, she was embarrassed. Because she never made a conscious decision to mentor young Rambo. That wasn't her intent. She had no idea because she was just doing what came naturally to her. She mothered me. She taught me. She gave birth to a small part of the world, and afterward I was able to leave her nest and thrive. That's how it's supposed to work. It's just natural.

I hope my sons meet women like that. Women who will help them on their journey. Because we need women. We're weak pathetic creatures. We can't do it on our own. And a mother's love will only take us so far.

But I'm clear-eyed. I know that women like my Globe-winning mentor are rare.

Women terrify me. They truly do. Women have a monstrous aspect that's concealed by their beauty. Helmut Newton captures this in his photos. His women are like creatures. Dangerous creatures. But at the same time, they're beautiful. They're alluring. You sense danger but you can't take your eyes off them. You're drawn to them. Despite the fear and despite the danger you still need them. Because men need women.

It's a cliché but it's as simple as that—men need women.

And so the thing that truly terrifies me is that my sons will end up hating and resenting women. Because that's no way for a man to live. Because men need women. They were made for us and we were made to love them.

A man who doesn't need them, or thinks he doesn't need them, is a defective. Maybe that's harsh but it's true. Because going through life hating and resenting half of humanity is no way to live. I don't care if the hatred stems from misogyny or faggotry—it's no way to live.

Hatred is poison. Even if you're right, even if you have empirical evidence that you're right, even if you're justified in your hatred, it's still poison. And I don't want my children to carry that with them.

My sons are going to need women—in ways that go far beyond sexual gratification. They're going to love women. Because I'm not going to let them be defective.

Sadly the deck is stacked against young men. The education system especially. If you need proof just look at college graduation rates where women now vastly outnumber men.

My son didn't get yelled at about a cat drawing. He got yelled at because he showed initiative. He showed creativity. It's just his nature. That's what he strives to do. I hope one day he'll strive to be a provider and protector.

But there's an entire system that also wants to be provider and protector. Some people refer to this as Socialism, with the American public education system at its vanguard. But I think it's something else. It's something new. Something we don't have a name for yet.

It's the Devouring Mother, but it's industrialized and manageri-alized and well financed. It's also networked—it spans the globe. It sees everything and records everything. It also judges every-thing. Because this strange beast is moral. This beast cares.

The best name I've heard is from the English writer Paul Kingsnorth who calls it "The Machine to Replace God." So for lack of a better word, let's call it The Machine.

The Machine sees young men as a threat. And it sees creative men as especially dangerous. Because creative men change the world. They imagine what the world should be. They imagine new realities. Then they make that new reality a concrete thing that you can touch and feel. Men have always done this.

As such, the art teacher, an apparatchik of The Machine, saw fit to raise her voice at my son for being creative. Because creative boys turn into creative men and creative men threaten the ascendency of The Machine. The art teacher knows her role. It's to shape young minds—shape them to fit seamlessly into The Machine.

My son knows something is amiss. Because he instinctively knows he didn't do anything wrong. He was given a task, real-ized it was stupid and pointless, and did something better. He did something praiseworthy. But instead of praise he received derision. And he couldn't understand why.

I don't blame him. It's bewildering. I would have come home crying too.

I didn't know how to explain it to him. I started by talking about the concept of the Longhouse, and gynocratic communal societies run by old hags. But this was over his head. I wasn't getting anywhere.

So instead I said he has to suffer through until he can go out on his own and build his own world like I had. I told him his job was to survive it. He just had to survive it. And I told him I would help, and that his mother would too. Because we love him.

I know he's not going to adapt and he's going to keep butting heads with teachers. I know this because I know him too well.

I know him too well because he's too much like me. And I wasn't able to adapt.

The Machine isn't going to let him succeed, no matter how hard he tries. I wasn't able to succeed until I left the system and dropped out of high school. I emancipated myself, and it was one of the best things I ever did.

But I didn't make it all the way out. Because thirty years later I was sitting there at a Dairy Queen eating soft serve and still dealing with the exact same issues.

In the past we offered to homeschool him, but he wasn't interested. He wanted to be with his friends. And his experience with homeschooling during the pandemic was disastrous. The isolation was terrible. Nothing saps the soul like loneliness.

But we'll find something he can succeed at. He needs to know what it's like to succeed. I don't know what that something will be, but we'll find it.

I tell myself that I'm not worried. That we'll figure this out. That he'll be fine.

But I am worried.

I looked at the junkies from the bus. They were still milling about. And I thought about my own history with addiction. I pictured my son getting off that bus, bubbling and popping, with a backpack full of god knows what, and I saw him with those vacant eyes.

He's going to love drugs. Because they dull the pain of living with The Machine.

I know this.

And I worry.

But maybe I can teach him. Maybe I can give him something he likes better than drugs. And maybe if he's armed with certain knowledge, he'll do better than I did. Maybe he'll escape farther than I was able to go.

Maybe he can make it all the way out.

TECH SCOUT

My favorite movie scene, maybe in all of cinema, is from Martin Scorsese's *Goodfellas*. It's the scene when Henry (played by the great Ray Liotta) takes his future wife Karen (Lorraine Bracco) to the Copacabana. But instead of entering through the front door he takes her down the stairs to the secret VIP entrance. They wind their way through the kitchen to the stage where a table is flown in just for them.

Aside from being technically brilliant, the scene is incredibly seductive. Henry is showing Karen his world, and in the process, he's also showing her how the world really works. She sees what happens in the back-of-house, and how access is granted by personal relationships and the greasing of palms. Karen eats it up. She starts the scene skeptical of Henry, but by the end of the scene she's in love.

One of the many cool things about my job is going behind the scenes of places that most people never see. I've seen more back-of-house entrances than I care to remember (and no, it's not because I'm a high roller, that's just how we get crews in and out of busy hotels, clubs, and restaurants).

You meet interesting people and learn fascinating things in these places, and sometimes you get a glimpse into how the world really works.

It's seductive.

We were scouting a farm in the Central Valley about three hours north of LA. We needed a farm and ranch location for a TV show and this was the place. The Central Valley is sixty miles at its widest point and runs four hundred and fifty miles from Redding in the north to just south of Bakersfield. At eighteen-thousand square miles it's about the size of Slovakia and is the heart of California's agriculture industry.

It was maybe 8:30 a.m., but it was already hot and dusty. And the dust in the Valley never goes away.

This was a "technical scout," more commonly abbreviated to "tech scout" or simply "the tech." This is when the key members of the crew gather at a location to figure out their game plan. The director explains his creative vision and the crew figures out how to execute it.

In this case, in addition to the key crew members and me (the unit production manager), we had a small contingent of writers, producers, and executives.

The farm was huge, one of the biggest in California and maybe the world. Our guide, one of the farm PR guys, said the place was about the same acreage as the state of Delaware (though it wasn't a contiguous piece of property).

Our tour started at the side of a dusty dirt road next to an almond orchard. There were trucks driving by, one every fifteen seconds.

Our tour guide, shouting over the roar of the trucks, said: "What you see behind me," and he pointed to the road and the trucks, "is the harvesting of eighty percent of the Italian tomato market for 20xx."

All of our hands shot up at the same time. Did you say eighty percent of the *Italian* tomato market?

He explained: over the next seventy-two hours, working three shifts a day, this farm would pick eighty percent of the tomatoes consumed in Italy for that year. He told us that these tomatoes had a mold content higher than what's allowed in the United States. However, the Italians think that a high mold content makes a better tomato, and they were eager to buy them.

We were silent. One after another, the trucks passed by. Giant plastic bins filled to the brim with tomatoes. There was a red slick on the dirt road where tomatoes had bounced out of the trucks and been crushed. The shoulder was full of broken tomatoes. We were imagining this parade of tomatoes twenty-four hours a day for the next three days. A truck every fifteen seconds, and it was all going to Italy.

Sometimes you get a glimpse into how the world really works. And how it's counterintuitive and strange. I'd read about globalization—I even talked about it quite a bit. What does it take to ship eighty percent of Italy's tomatoes from California? It must take thousands of trucks and dozens (if not hundreds) of container ships.

An enormous operation. And though I was watching it happen, I couldn't comprehend it. I couldn't quite believe it.

Later, when I was alone with our guide, I asked about those little expensive boxes of Italian tomatoes I buy at Whole Foods. Were they grown in California?

He said, yes, they most likely were California tomatoes but it depends on the year and the weather and many other factors. But more often than not, Italian tomatoes are not grown in Italy. They're grown (and partially processed) in California, then shipped to Italy, then repackaged and shipped back to the USA.

I also asked him why Italy has to import tomatoes—it seemed implausible. The first thing I think of when I think of Italy is tomato. He told me they can't grow enough of them to come even close to meet domestic demand.

And then he told me that most countries can't grow enough food, period. He said, "We feed the world."

He was very proud of that fact, and I don't blame him. It's a good mission to have.

They had a restaurant on the farm. Actually they had several. The restaurants, little cafés really, aren't open to the public. And they're not there for the farm workers. They exist solely to feed the farm's global clientele.

The lunchroom was crowded and I couldn't find a seat, so I asked some Argentinian gentlemen if I could join them. They said they were buyers from the South American Nut Cartel. I could tell they were waiting for the joke, so I said something about how excited I was to make a cartel connection. They laughed. We had a good lunch.

I had the pozole. It was excellent. Maybe the best I've ever had. The ingredients were fresh. All grown on the farm, said the chef.

There was no charge. Farm clients get a free lunch.

As we ate, the guys from the cartel explained that they were buying almonds for Argentina. Because Argentina, just like Italy and tomatoes, can't produce enough almonds to meet demand. So they come to California.

If you've ever seen the inside of a peach pit you've seen a thing at the center that looks like an almond. It actually is an almond, but not quite. And whatever you do, please don't eat it. You'll find that it's bitter and full of cyanide.

Almonds are a close genetic cousin to the peach. But they've been bred to taste sweet and have less cyanide. On the branch they look like a withered peach without that delicious peachy flesh. Each tree produces about fifty pounds of nuts each year.

But to get that fifty pounds of nuts you have to give the tree a lot of water. The figures are insane. They say it takes just over three gallons of water for each almond. That's not per tree, that's three gallons per nut.

▱▱▱▱

South of the California Delta (where this particular farm was located) they need four acre/feet of water per acre of almond trees per year. So imagine an orchard, then imagine it's flooded with chest-deep water. That's how much water it takes.

California's Central Valley used to be the American Serengeti. Just a large hot arid grassland. But every year snowmelt from the Sierra Nevada would flood the plain, which caused an explosion in animal and plant life. The old accounts say there were so many birds they would black out the sun. The rivers were full of salmon and steelhead. After going out to sea and circling the Pacific Ocean, the salmon would return every year to spawn in the rivers and tributaries—sometimes all the way to the summit of the Sierras.

There used to be a fishing industry in the Central Valley. There were salmon canneries in Sacramento and all over the California Delta. But then came the dams. The salmon lost access to their spawning grounds. The runs stopped and the canneries went out of business.

Dam building began in earnest during the Great Depression. The goal was flood control—and to create jobs. But in the 1960s California launched the State Water Plan (SWP), a public works project to build dams, reservoirs, and irrigation canals on a scale Roman engineers could never have imagined.

The SWP brought water to previously arid areas. Land that used to be desert was suddenly productive. There was enough water to flood an almond orchard with four acre/feet of water every year.

With ample water, desert sun, and chemical fertilizer, California became the vegetable fruit and nut basket of the world. And then the global population boomed. And then trade barriers fell. And suddenly, in the year I visited that farm, eighty percent of the tomatoes eaten in Italy were grown in California by an imported workforce.

And yes, there was a workforce. A large one.

They told me, and though I forget the exact number, it was substantial. And that didn't include seasonal (and migrant) workers. It takes thousands of people to run something this large.

Most of the workers were Latino. Some were new, some had been there for generations. This land used to be Mexico after all.

The migrant workers, the ones that did the picking, looked indigenous. A lot of them spoke Spanish as a second language. The historic languages of Mesoamerica were their native tongue.

But the full-time workers, the ones that run and fix the equipment, do the planting, and manage the irrigation, they were Mestizo: descendants of the Spanish colonialists who took native brides. They're good people. Happy, content people. And they're good workers. They're good at their jobs—like the chef who made my pozole.

Unlike the fiercely independent and sometimes surly working-class Anglos, the Mestizos are pleasant and compliant: they do what they're told.

"The best farmers in the world," said my Sonoma-vineyard-owning buddy when talking about his workers.

Campesino. It means farmer, but it can also mean "peasant." My Spanish-speaking friends say the literal translation is something like "from the land" or "belonging to the land"—or it just means "farmer." I guess it depends on the context.

The "belonging to the land" translation might be the best way to describe these people. Because when this farm is sold—when it inevitably changes hands—the workers will stay. They belong to the land.

We scouted a big part of the property. We found what we were going to film and figured out how we were going to film it and what we would need to get the job done—but I was still figuring out how to pay for it all.

The thing that struck me as we toured the farm was its vastness. As far as you could see there was nothing but cultivation. Eventually we came across a rocky outcrop, which we climbed to the top of to see if it would make a good establishing shot. From there, the entire farm was laid out before us. Actually, the entire Central Valley. I could see the snow-capped peaks of the Sierras.

The sheer size of the farm was disturbing. I'm an outdoorsman. I'm used to being alone in vast spaces surrounded by nature—places not touched by man. This place was vast, but it wasn't natural.

Nothing but cultivation. I had seen farms, but not like this. It was too big. Too much unnaturalness.

But I was impressed by the efficiency. Everything was accounted for. Every gallon of water, every pound of fertilizer, every tank of diesel fuel—they could tell you exactly how much they used that day.

And nothing went to waste. For example, they take the husks of the almond (the peach that's not quite a peach) and feed it to cattle. When an almond grove has reached the end of its lifespan (and almond trees have a lifespan—about twenty-five years) they grind up the tree and use it as mulch.

Like the Plains Indians who were said to use every part of the buffalo, the operators of this farm were both efficient and frugal. And I'm always impressed by frugality.

We spent the night at Harris Ranch. You've seen it if you've driven Interstate 5 between LA and San Francisco. Harris Ranch is at the halfway point. Colloquially known as "Cow-schwitz," it's still a working cattle concern. On any given day the feedlot could be home to as many as 120,000 beeves. You can smell it from miles away.

The cattle spend their first two years grazing on a local ranch, then they're moved to the feedlot for "finishing," where they're fed a diet of grain and alfalfa hay to put on fat and marble the meat.

"Grass fed, grain finished" is my favorite kind of beef, but it's disturbing when you see (and smell) it at an industrial scale.

Aside from the agribusiness, Harris Ranch operates a restaurant and hotel on Interstate 5. The restaurant is decent, and the hotel is nice. I wouldn't call it a four-star hotel, but the Automobile Association of America (AAA) gives it a five diamond rating (its highest).

I sat down for a steak dinner with the team. I was still drinking in those days and they had a great wine list. I ordered the prime rib smoked over oak coals. Beef cooked on oak, sometimes known as Santa Maria Barbecue, is a Central California specialty. It goes back to the rancheria days when California was at the fringes of the Spanish Empire. They had cattle and they had oak and that's how they cooked their beef.

The next day we were going to scout another ranch that supplied Harris Ranch with its beef—the place where our dinner was born and raised. I could sense some discomfort from the team when the steaks arrived. They were anticipating meeting the relatives of their dinner.

The other ranch—where the Harris beef is raised—is in Parkfield, California. As of 2024, the population was eighteen. The nearest gas station is an hour in any direction. It might be the most remote municipality in California.

Parkfield is famous for two things. One, it's where actor James Dean died after crashing his Porsche 550 Spyder there in 1955. The second thing is earthquakes. The town sits on the San Andreas Fault and is one of the most earthquake-prone places in the world. It's a popular destination for geology students and hobbyists.

We had a location manager to show us the way, but he was a worthless political hire and kept getting lost. So I called the ranch matron and got directions before we lost cell service outside of Coalinga. The route involved many miles of unpaved backroads. She warned me to watch out for migrating tarantulas.

I thought she was joking. She wasn't.

We were in a caravan of SUVs. I was driving the second car back. All the cars had film industry walkie-talkies so we could stay in touch. The caravan had left the valley and entered the hills that separate the Central Valley from the coast.

The walkie clicked on and I heard "OH MY GOD!" as the car in front of us screeched to a halt in a cloud of dust.

I asked what was wrong. The walkie clicks on again and all I hear is screeching women. And then I saw it.

In front of the lead SUV, a tarantula was dragging a dead bird across the road. We waited for the spider to pass, the girls in the lead car got it together, and we kept going toward the ranch.

There's no law in Parkfield. Not that I'd call it a lawless place, but there's no cop within an hour's drive so people have to solve their own problems. And because there's no one around to enforce silly rules and regulations, the residents don't follow them.

The lawless nature of Parkfield was illustrated shortly after we got to the ranch. We were in front of the house saying hello to the ranch matron. As we were exchanging pleasantries, we saw a dust plume heading toward us.

The matron said, "That's my youngest coming home from school." There's a one-room schoolhouse in Parkfield. It's about a twenty-minute drive from the ranch.

I asked what grade she was in. The matron said sixth grade. I said, oh that makes her about twelve and gosh that's a wonderful age.

As we're having the conversation the truck turns down the long driveway. It was a Ford F-350 crew cab—a big truck for big jobs. It has a 4-ton payload capacity. I could hear the engine now. It was a big diesel. Big trucks need big engines.

And then I started to wonder who was driving that big truck. The matron had already mentioned that her husband was out of town—he was a lobbyist for the ranching industry and spent most of his time in Washington, DC. Oh, it must be another parent then, I thought. Got it.

But then the truck came to a stop, the driver's door opened, and out climbed . . . a twelve-year-old girl.

California is the most over-regulated and over-legalized state in the USA. They love passing new laws—laws that nobody needs or asked for.

But in Parkfield they don't care about silly regulations that say a kid can't drive before they turn sixteen. How else are the kids supposed to get to school? The parents are running cattle ranches, and running a cattle ranch is hard. They don't have time for school drop off. Just let her take the damn truck.

With the husband absent in DC the ranch was run by the matron and her two daughters along with what I remember as one ranch hand. I forget the acreage but, like the farm from the previous day, the place was huge. I believe she said it was the size of Manhattan, which puts it at about twenty-two square miles.

And even though it's the size of the island of Manhattan, the ranch was only home to five people. The family settled the land in the 1790s when it was still part of the Spanish Empire. The land may have been granted to them by a Habsburg king, but they still had to trek into the wilderness and fight Native Americans and deal with a multitude of deprivations at what was then the end of the known world.

After two centuries of intermarriage they looked Anglo. They spoke English at home, they had an Anglo name, and they acted like Anglos. These weren't Campesinos. These people were landed aristocrats.

These were cattlemen, ranchers, herdsmen, graziers, pastoralists, whatever you want to call them. But the current technical term, the one I'm sure her lobbyist husband used, is "Livestock Producer."

The matron gave us a tour in her SUV. She had Valley Fever and wore a bandanna to keep the dust out of her lungs.

Valley Fever, also known as coccidioidomycosis, is a respiratory disease prevalent in the Central Valley. It's caused by the spores of the Coccidioides immitis fungus. The fungus lives in the soil, but it gets kicked into the air by the large-scale tilling of the Central Valley factory farms. And if you breathe the dust long enough, you're going to get it.

The matron was driving, which allowed me to take in the scenery. It's one of the most beautiful places I've been. Golden grass with green California live oaks dotting the rolling hills. And very little sign of the hand of man. Aside from the two-track ranch road there were no other signs of development and the modern world.

Quail were running all over the road in front of the SUV. I joked that I would take care of her quail infestation free of charge.

I like quail. I like eating it and I like hunting it—just like I did when I was a kid growing up in the mountains at the edge of the Great Basin. I'm angling for a hunting invite.

She just said, "Ah, so he has a taste for quail," and left it at that. She didn't want some retard from LA stumbling around her land with a shotgun. She wasn't exactly wrong, and I never got the hunting invite.

We saw deer and we saw elk and we saw cattle. Thousands and thousands of cattle. They were doing what cattle do best: eating grass and chewing cud. Ruminants are really a miracle of nature. They eat things humans can't (grass) and turn it into something we can (meat).

And this is how they're supposed to live. Free to roam, to eat what they want when they want it. No hormones, no antibiotics (unless they're sick—she was very clear about that).

She said she sells all of her beeves to Harris Ranch. Harris sells beef under its own label but they also supply all the ground beef for the In-N-Out Burger restaurant chain.

I told her In-N-Out was my favorite (this is true). She said she'd never had it. I was shocked and asked why.

She said she never eats the beef she raises. While she does eat beef, she won't eat her own beef. Because she loves her animals too much, she said.

The director wanted a hill with an oak tree at the top. So the ranch matron took us to a hill she liked and we parked at the base. At that time there was no cell-phone service at the ranch. A production manager without cell service is dead in the water. There was no one to call, no equipment to order, no quotes to solicit, no numbers to crunch. With nothing to add to the process, I sat on the tailgate of the SUV while the team climbed the hill.

Before she left to join the team, the matron pointed out a bull elk who'd adopted a harem of bovine cows. I sat and watched him as the team did their thing up the hill.

Bull elk have harems of elk cows that they jealously guard. When a young bull reaches sexual maturity he'll try to mate with one of daddy bull's harem. A fight ensues. But the young elk is small and weak and inevitably loses. He's driven out of the herd and has to live on his own without the herd's protection until he's big enough and strong enough to fight for and win a harem of his own.

This elk, however, was Sigma. Instead of following the normal path of living alone and afraid in a hostile world he decided to create a harem of she-beeves. The bovine cows took him in just like they would have taken in a bovine bull. And there he was living contentedly, sitting under a tree while his harem of beeves silently grazed in the California sun.

Maybe one day he'll get big enough to fight a mature bull. And maybe he'll get lonely for his own kind and fight for and win his own cow elk. Maybe his new lady friends will get turned into Double-Double Animal Style. But not today. It wasn't rutting season and today he seemed content.

The team was taking a long time up on the hill. I didn't care. I sat there watching the elk and his harem, and the trees, and the rolling hills, and the grass and the wind.

The sun started getting low and the world got extra gold. The sun really races across the sky. It's not something you notice when you're looking at a phone.

One time I was the assistant director (AD) on a non-union shoot. The AD is like a crew chief. I was there to keep things running, to keep things moving. We were trying for a magic hour shot—trying to catch the fleeting golden light that happens just before sunset. The crew was moving slow so I said (as I'd said hundreds of times before), "Hurry up guys, the sun is moving."

Some fat second camera assistant lacking in urgency snarked, "Don't you mean 'hurry up the earth is turning'?" Har har har.

He was new. Fresh out of film school. I think he was someone's nephew.

Somehow he got through four years of film school without learning that film work is a blue-collar job. We get shit done. Because if we don't get shit done, we'll all get fired and someone else will get it done and you'll be working at a video store because that's all your film degree qualifies you to do. So check your intellect at the door and get to work, fatty.

I told him, "Actually, we're planted here. And we're not going anywhere. But the sun is. So move the fucking lens case out of the shot before the sun moves."

And that's where I was now. I was planted. I wasn't going anywhere. I wasn't moving but the sun was. It's an old way to look at the world. It's a better way to look at the world. It's a way that makes sense.

I was the center of the world, and the universe was moving around me.

And that's how I was in that moment, as I sat on the tailgate of the SUV while the golden sun dipped toward the horizon. I was still, and content. Just like my elk friend.

DAY OFF

My dad didn't tell me stories. He didn't talk about himself. And most of the stories he could have told me, I was too young to hear. I got those later, after he died, second-hand—a relative gifting me possessions of a dead man.

What he did tell me was practical stuff. About how to write down important things in code, like bank account numbers. And how to comb my hair and talk to a barber. And how to play craps.

He was an old man by the time I was born. And he was even older when I was growing up. Because we're all getting older, and we're all getting closer to death.

Being older, I don't know if he knew how to relate to me. His wife (my stepmother), a twenty-something model, did know how to relate to me. Because at that young age she still remembered how to be a kid. She gave the best birthday presents—she knew what the kids were into.

But as she spiraled into addiction, I would see her less and less on my visits. She'd be at "camp," which is what my dad called rehab, or she'd go into the master bedroom and not come out for the entirety of my stay.

One way my father communicated was through movies. On my frequent visits to LA, we'd see a movie every night. He lived in Beverly Hills, so we'd usually hit the theaters in Westwood.

It was such a joy to see the Bruin Theater in *Once Upon a Time in Hollywood* because I'd seen so many films there as a child. But as an adult who lived in LA off and on for the better part of two decades, I never saw a film there.

I considered it many times, but I'd think about my dad and all the questions I wish I would have asked him. Then I'd think about my childhood, about the uncertainty and the loneliness and the hunger.

Then I'd remember the time my mother took me to see him before he died. I was there to say goodbye to my dad. He was living with an old girlfriend in a condo on Wilshire. Some other family members were there. Female family members. And I'd remember how they treated us—the contempt they had for my mother and the pity they had for me.

Then I'd remember his funeral a few weeks later, and not knowing what to do with myself. And I'd remember sitting shiva at a house in Beverly Hills. I had a Walkman and a tape of REM's *Green* and I listened to it over and over again because in my pain and confusion I didn't know what else to do.

It was too painful to go to that theater. I couldn't go back.

My dad loved movies. And it wasn't just a hobby, it was a major part of his life's work as an entertainment attorney.

He knew The Business, and he knew a lot of the players. He had represented many luminaries. Some of them were close personal friends. But his friends were passing away.

Because time and age does that.

There's a time in life when you go to birthday parties, then there's a time when you go to weddings. And then there's a time when you go to funerals. When I was a kid, he was going to a lot of funerals.

He had trouble connecting with his grade-school-age son, but that didn't stop him from trying. He'd try to come up with fun trips. Like Disneyland, or Knott's Berry Farm, or Magic Mountain.

Sometimes we would do destination stuff. He'd fly in, pick me up, and take me somewhere.

I remember a trip to the Breakers in Palm Beach. He also loved the Hotel Del in Coronado. He loved big classic luxury hotels. So we'd take these trips, and stay at these hotels, and then I'd go back to living in poverty with my mother with the food stamps and the government peaches and the government cheese.

It was a strange way to grow up.

I guess it would have been around 1985 when he started telling me about the New York World's Fair, and how he went as a young man, and how incredible it was. It sounded fantastic. The entire world showed up? And going to the fair was like seeing all the countries in the world? Amazing!

Then the next year, he sprang it on me. We were going to the World's Fair in Vancouver, BC, also known as Expo 86. I was thrilled. I was ready to see the future. I was ready to see the world.

But it sucked. It just fucking sucked.

It was rainy, it was cold, and it was boring as fuck.

The monorail was cool, but I'd been on one at Disneyland. I don't remember anything from the fair except that it was wet and that fucking monorail. I forget the exact date, but I feel like we must have been there toward the end of the fair because it was quiet and lifeless.

The city and the world had already moved on, ready to reclaim and redevelop the land into god knows what.

It felt like a cemetery. That emptiness. It was like walking through rainy ruins.

I was just a kid, but I wasn't impressed. I could tell my dad wasn't impressed either. We had come to see The Future.

In New York in 1939, The Future was still coming. By New York in 1964 and Montreal in 1967, the future had arrived. Men were in space. A better world was being built.

But by 1986 the future had stopped cold. It had stagnated. What we saw at the fair was a preview of the post-industrial malaise and hints of our current globalized dystopia.

My dad was as bored and disengaged as I was.

The highlight of the trip, however, was when we saw a movie. This was our thing. We were good at this. We liked this. We couldn't fuck this up. And the movie we saw was *Ferris Bueller's Day Off*.

⬛⬛⬛⬛

Of all the movies we saw together this is the one I remember the most vividly. Maybe because it was a welcome respite from our failed adventure. Maybe because this was before the cancer, and his drawn-out divorce, when Dad was still happy.

And maybe that's how I want to remember him. Not the broken man of a few years later living in a hotel and going bankrupt.

But mostly, it's because he loved that film. Of all the movies we'd seen together, he enjoyed that one the most. Afterward he was beaming. And I was too.

It's a fantastic film. I think it's the best of the 1980s, and maybe the best of all time. And this one changed us. It changed my dad, and it changed me.

Of course, great cinema has that effect. It has that power. You get hypnotized by the moving image. It's not real, it's just light reflected off a screen. But you think it's real.

I've said this before. I repeat it because it's true.

You don't look at a film, you look *into* it.

And it hypnotizes you.

And it implants ideas into you. Plants them deep. Most people don't even know they're there.

And those ideas change you.

If you think this sounds like the plot of Christopher Nolan's *Inception*, you are correct. Because this *is* the plot of *Inception*, which is a movie about how movies work.

Movies play with time and space and hypnotize and implant ideas. Movies can be insidious tools of propaganda. Some people intuit this, and they don't trust the film or the filmmakers. And then they come up with wild conspiracy theories (mostly involving Jews).

I don't blame these people. They're intelligent enough to know they've been somehow manipulated. They feel this. And they're trying to make sense of this.

But they don't have the wisdom to know that there's too much incompetence in the world for grand conspiracy. And they don't know the filmmakers just want you to enjoy the movie so the movie makes money so the powers that be let them make another movie.

Because they don't want to alter or control you. The filmmakers just want to make movies. It's what they love to do.

I'm going to assume you've seen *Ferris Bueller*, so I won't review the plot. But let me just say that it's deceptive. It's sneaky. And it's a shiv to the guts so slow and so deep that I didn't feel it for decades.

The key to the sleight of hand is this: it's not about Ferris.

It's about Cameron. He's the one with the character arc. He's the one who experiences genuine change. He starts the movie as a pathetic miserable young man without a future who'd be better off killing himself, and ends as a guy who might have a chance in life.

Ferris Bueller is the titular and most entertaining character. In fact, he's so entertaining it took me a long time to figure out that *Ferris Bueller* is not about Ferris Bueller. Ferris is merely the Mephistopheles to Cameron's Faust.

Cameron's Hero's Journey goes something like this:

Normal life: Cameron is "sick" in his parents' cold loveless home.

The Call to Adventure is Ferris asking him to help spring Ferris's girlfriend Sloane from school, which involves stealing the forbidden Ferrari.

Cameron crosses the threshold into the underworld as they leave school and drive into Chicago.

In Chicago they face many tests.

The final ordeal comes when Cameron realizes the Ferrari has racked up too many miles and that his father will notice it and punish him. He becomes catatonic from fear and falls into a pool. At which point he is reborn.

Finally, Cameron decides to destroy the Ferrari, take the blame, and stand up to his father. He decides to exercise agency over his own life, thus becoming "the master of both worlds."

I don't think John Hughes planned his story this way. I don't think it's possible to intentionally write something that subtle, that clever.

I think he was touched by the muse and this is what came out. This is how art happens.

The muse touches you and something comes out. I know because this is what happens to me. And I don't know where it comes from.

This is what I see when I watch the movie. This is what I see the muse told John Hughes to make. I see a story about a young man's journey through this hostile and unfair and irrational and absurd world.

But then again, I've gained some years now, and I have kids and responsibilities. And successes, and many failures. And things I'm proud of, and things that I'm still ashamed of. And many things I have yet to do.

But what did my father see on that rainy day in Vancouver? He left the theater transformed. He didn't know about the cancer yet, or that his wife was going to leave him and try to take him for everything. Or what to do with his young son from a middle marriage who would grow up without a father.

I'd like to think that he was thinking about me. That the movie gave him hope for me. That maybe I wasn't doomed. That maybe I'd turn out okay.

That's what I'd like to think, but I'm not sure it's true.

There are mundane things I wish I could ask my deceased loved ones, especially Mom and Dad.

Mundane things like, where did those Krugerrands in your safe deposit box come from, Mom? Or, how did you feel about *Ferris Bueller's Day Off*, Dad?

It would be nice to have those answers. But life doesn't give you the answers you want when you want them.

It's something I'll have to wait for.

INVISIBLE

Coming home was my favorite part.

I'd get the last flight out of LAX and land at 1 a.m. local time. Then I'd get my bags and my truck and I might be home by 2 or 2:30 a.m. But that drive home was awesome. You can drive fast that time of night, but more often than not, I'd get stuck at a railroad crossing.

My town is surrounded by railroad tracks, and they're always moving freight at night so I'd often get stuck. Just me and the crossing lights and the train. And the sound. The rhythmic sound of the wheels on the tracks. It's quiet here at night. Things sound different. Everything is more clear, less muddled.

The train was a reminder that I wasn't in LA anymore and I could let the stress go. I could downshift. I was home. And better yet, nobody knew who I was.

━━━━

It's amazing how many existential issues are solved by having a child. You hold that little thing—that little baby—and you know what you have to do. The fatherly instinct kicks in and you know your purpose is to take care of this child, you have to raise him right. And you have to do a better job than the people who raised you.

Being a dad seemed simple, but it wasn't simple. And it wasn't easy either.

When my wife got pregnant, neither of us wanted to raise kids in LA. Also, she worked as a costumer, and her hours were crazy. You can't do that job and be any sort of mom.

We briefly tried the Bay Area. We'd met in San Francisco, and her family was there. We thought we could make it work in The City if we had family support.

We had a great little cottage in The Sunset. Very charming but small.

Then she got pregnant with our second, and we needed more space. But we couldn't afford the space in The City. We'd have to go to Sacramento to afford something larger.

So I thought, If I'm going to commute four hours a day, why not just fly in?

Then I started doing the math. We could pay cash for a house in a mountain state, I could fly back to LA for work and spend two weeks a month in four-star hotels, and it would still be cheaper than buying anywhere in California.

So that's what we did. We left California.

I had grown up in the mountains, and that's where I wanted to raise my kids. My wife was from an ultra-rural part of the Central Valley, and she was okay with small-town life. And me commuting back to Cali would only be until I could find a job closer to home.

The town where we settled wasn't exactly small. It's more like a small city. But it was the smallest place I had lived in all my adult life. I fell in love.

I fell in love with the people, and the big trees, and the old houses, and riding my bike through the countryside, and trout fishing close to home, and our little neighborhood park pond filled with bass and bluegill.

The house we bought wasn't a palace, but it was good enough for our young family. And with the cost of living my wife could stay at home with the kids. Things were perfect.

Perfect, except that I soon learned the constant commuting wasn't sustainable. It was exhausting. Sometimes I'd fly down and back in the same day. But often I'd leave for LA late-night Sunday and come home late-night Friday. I flew so often I was on a first-name basis with the flight crews.

My children were growing up without me. Not only was I missing milestones like birthdays and new words and first visits from the tooth fairy, I was denying them the stabilizing presence of a father. It was something I didn't have growing up, and I was determined that it would be different for my kids.

All I needed to do was find a job closer to home. But I couldn't find one. It turned out that nobody wanted me.

As both a high-school and a college dropout, my only credentials were a GED and years of experience in an industry no one understands.

I applied for all sorts of jobs. I started with advertising agencies, thinking my commercial production experience would carry over, but I couldn't even get an interview. Then I tried marketing firms but got the same result. Then project management, then construction management. I even applied for retail jobs at sporting-goods stores. If I was lucky enough to get an interview, they would tell me I was "overqualified"—which meant I wasn't qualified at all.

Also, by that point in my career, I desperately wanted out of The Business. It wasn't just the commuting. It was the whole thing. The pressure, the hours, the crazy people. They had all taken their toll. There was a numbness inside of me—a feeling that all my hard work, all my sacrifices, were somehow meaningless.

As I've said, there's no glamor when you're on the inside looking out. It's just a job. Just a profession. Just a lot of hard, stressful work.

But I kept going. I had no other choice.

To maintain my sanity and avoid having a breakdown, I began telling myself certain "truths." That, actually, I loved my job! That it was fun and exciting!

This allowed me to keep it together. To not crack. In the meantime, I told myself to stop being a pussy and to suck it up until I could find something better.

But deep down I knew I was cracking and that I had to get out. I was in a crazy situation. It was absurd.

And soon I found myself in a darkly comedic place. Every time I'd get on that plane for work, I would secretly hope for my death. Hope that the plane would go down in a ball of fire with me in it.

There's a scene in David Fincher's Fight Club where the Edward Norton character, burned out by his soulless job and exhausted by constant business travel, imagines himself dying in a mid-air collision. My fantasies were very similar.

As I sat in my seat, readying for takeoff, I would put on my headphones and play the music I wanted to die to. Usually Led Zeppelin, or something else heavy and epic. When the plane turned onto the runway, and when I could feel the takeoff thrust and noise and vibration—that's when the movie in my head would roll.

A common fantasy was that the plane would hit a flock of Canadian geese. There'd be a quick series of clunking noises outside the windows and a blinding burst of feathers. Then the engines would catch fire and the plane would bank sharply. Smoke would fill the cabin and I'd see flames outside the windows as the miracle of commercial aviation devolved into a grotesque nightmare of tragedy and pain and death and destruction and the sweet cleansing fire of burning jet fuel.

And while everyone would be screaming and praying and crying, I would be calmly waiting for the end. I was ready for this. I had been ready for this my whole life. And, with maybe just a hint of a smile on my face, I'd sit there stoically rocking out to Robert Plant singing "Ramble On" as the ground rapidly approached.

As absurd as all of this was, the truth was that I really would not have cared if the plane went down. My spirit was numb. I was ready to surrender. I just wanted out.

In Fight Club, Edward Norton invented the Tyler Durden persona to cope. I didn't create an imaginary alter ego to save myself. My mind wasn't that broken, I guess. Instead I plodded on—feebly and obediently.

It was a dark place. I stayed there for many years.

●●●●●

The airplane, as you probably have guessed, never went down. Instead it would make it to LA or whatever city I was shooting in.

As soon as the wheels hit the tarmac, I'd turn on my phone. Today a producer's primary tool is Zoom, but at that time it was the phone. And mine would ring nonstop.

There were so many calls to make and take. So much information to organize—preproduction is all about gathering, collating, and distributing information to the relevant crew members. Then there are people to hire, stages to book, and budgets to manage. Maybe I'd have to talk down a director who was panicking, or maybe soothe an agent who thought her client was getting screwed, or chew out a vendor who was trying to fuck me on a rental contract.

Nobody knows what a producer does. Even people in The Business don't understand.

This is partly due to there being many types of producers. For example, in broadcast television, like what you see on CNN, the person called a "producer" is more like what I would call a director. But in my world, a producer serves a different role.

The best analogy is from the construction industry. If a director is like an architect, then a producer is like a general contractor. The director handles the creative aspects, while the producer takes care of the nuts-and-bolts stuff—like logistics, hiring the crew, renting equipment, and negotiating contracts.

There's a lot to worry about. A producer is responsible for every facet of the production. My résumé says something like "ensures project delivery is on time and on budget while maintaining the highest standards of creative quality." Which basically means I get the job done while hitting the impossible trifecta of good, fast, and cheap.

Still, there were myriad ways that things could (and did) go south. Even if it wasn't my fault, even if it was something completely out of my control, it was still my problem, and I had to fix it. Problems within my control were easy—I simply fixed them before they became a problem. But problems out of my control were another story. That's where things got sticky.

●●●●●

When I lived in San Francisco I joined a fly-fishing club. They have a lovely little clubhouse in Golden Gate Park; it might be the prettiest part of the park. As a community service, we'd teach injured GWOT vets to fly fish. On these trips they'd sometimes tell us about their experiences in the war, including their injuries—physical and otherwise.

There was a woman who was at Fallujah, just like my Marine buddy. She was a former Army MP who had a TBI (traumatic brain injury) as well as a serious case of PTSD.

She had trouble being around large groups of people and couldn't handle being in any sort of town, large or small, so she lived by herself in a rural part of the Sierra Foothills. Even our small group of anglers was too much for her to handle.

She told me the issue was control—that in normal life there were "too many variables." She felt the need to control everything and everyone, because that's what she had to do to survive in Iraq. And she would panic when she was in situations she couldn't control, like a long line at the grocery store, or in a crowded bar, or even walking down a busy sidewalk.

I felt the same thing when the plane landed at LAX. There were too many variables, too many things beyond my control, too many things that could go wrong. It would all come rushing at me at once. It was overwhelming.

But I didn't panic. I was known for being calm and levelheaded under pressure. In fact, I would do a funny thing: the crazier things got, the calmer I'd get. As I was coming up in the production department as a production manager and coordinator, this eccentricity would drive my bosses crazy. They wanted me to be as freaked out as they were.

For me as a producer, the calmness helped. It was an asset. It allowed me, as a leader of the production, to keep the entire crew calm. It was like hitting them with a tuning fork, and all of us vibing at the same composed frequency. We'd all be calm and levelheaded and convinced we were going to get through this and no one would get freaked out or yelled at. The crews appreciated this. They liked working for me.

But this was all for show. The calmness I projected was just a facade. I kept cool on the outside, but inside I was struggling. The stress and anxiety of the job, which I kept hidden from everyone around me, began to grow and accumulate, taking up more of my spirit, more of my soul.

Then I would drink. Because it helped.

I'd be filled with stress and anxiety and countless fears—fear that I would screw something up, fear that the phone would stop ringing, fear that I would not be able to support my family, fear of sitting home alone all day with my thoughts and that little voice in my head telling me I am and always have been a failure.

But after a few drinks I'd feel better. I'd get through the day. Yet, as time went on, it took more and more booze or pills or whatever else I could find to relax my fears and stop that little voice in my head.

And then one day the booze stopped working. It didn't work at all. I would still get drunk, but it didn't give me the desired effect. No amount of alcohol would make me feel better.

Still, I kept drinking. I couldn't stop. I'd lost control. And then I reached the point where the only way I would stop was when I could no longer get the glass to my mouth.

Many times I tried to stop, but I repeatedly failed. I went back to the bottle, again and again, and each time things got significantly worse.

"Out of control" is a perfect way to phrase it. Imagine you're driving down a winter road and you think things are fine. But you go down a hill and realize you're on ice. You hit the brakes, but instead of slowing down the tires lock up and you start to accelerate. You're sliding downhill—sliding out of control.

For me, the realization of being out of control was accompanied by sheer terror. It was intolerable, a feeling of extreme hopelessness and constant panic. And I was ready to do anything to make it stop—including ending my life.

They call that rock bottom. But rather than ending my life, I found AA, and I got sober.

Along the way, I learned a few lessons. One is that life doesn't stop when you stop drinking. Another is that things don't always get better. Sometimes they get worse.

I know this because things got worse for me. All my problems were still there, but I could no longer use alcohol as a crutch. All the stress, all the pressure—it was still there. And now I had no way to deal with it. Not like before anyway, not like when I had the magic bullet of a belt of scotch.

As I've said, it's important not to fuck up in this business, because each new fuckup could be your last. And I was constantly terrified of fucking up.

Making things worse, there are countless ways to do this—to fuck up. Such as forgetting to order a minor but critical piece of equipment, or failing to properly convert the set dimensions sent by a European production designer from metric measurements to inches and feet, or scheduling talent to arrive at the wrong time of day, or even on the wrong day.

Another way to fuck up is to mentally snap and act out. We all have our limits. A person can only handle a finite amount of stress and exhaustion and bullshit. And when the limit is hit, something happens and people just crack. They break wide open.

I'd seen it happen countless times. And in the past, I'd done it myself.

Back in my PA days, I performed many tasks. I did work both on and off set. The off-set work included chauffeuring VIPs visiting from out of town—directors, producers, and actors. For many PAs, this is a typical assignment.

Oftentimes, it can be a terrifying ordeal—for both the PA and the passenger. The problem is that the PA is afraid of making a mistake. So they fixate on everything that can go wrong and, inevitably, because they are fixating on everything that can go wrong, something goes wrong. At which point the feared thing happens: the big shot in the backseat starts yelling at the cowering PA. Sometimes there's even an epic meltdown.

I know this because it happened to me. Many times over.

And it kept happening to me until another PA gave me some advice. He said the thing to do when someone is screaming in a car is to drive like a fucking maniac. Floor it and weave in and out of traffic and run lights and make the tires squeal. And, most importantly, don't say a word. Don't say a fucking word.

The point is to remind the screaming egomaniac that they are mortal and that one day—maybe today—they are going to die. That would stop the screaming.

I laughed off that advice. It seemed absurd.

But one day I was tasked with driving Big-Shot British Director. It was the last day of filming and his wife had flown in from the UK and he was meeting her for dinner. The production coordinator gave me an address and written directions (this was before smartphones and in-car navigation) and I went to get the car.

I hadn't talked to this guy the entire shoot. He was a good director. I enjoyed watching him work, but I thought it odd that he wore a suit and tie on set.

As he got in the backseat of the rental SUV, I opened with a friendly, "Hi. How's it going?" Because I'm an easygoing American, and we're going to have a great time on the way to the restaurant, right?

But if there's one thing the Brits know, it's how to treat their inferiors—in this case, a twentysomething PA.

Ignoring my greeting, Big-Shot said, "Do you know where you're going?" His tone was snooty and proper, like an English lord, though on set it had gone around that his accent was a product of elocution lessons meant to obscure his modest origins.

I answered, "Uh, yes I do."

"Carry on then."

He might as well have added "chop-chop," as if I were some rickshaw driver in a third-world malarial port city.

I thought, Okay, he doesn't want to talk. Fine. I'm a pro. Let's just get this guy to dinner.

Unlike a lot of PA chauffeurs, I was a confident driver. I wasn't worried. And on this particular drive, there wasn't a lot that could go wrong.

Except, things did go wrong. For starters, I took him to the wrong restaurant. The place had a similar name as the one I was given, but it was a dive in a seedy part of LA. As soon as we saw it we both knew there had been a mistake. Then his wife called him. She was wondering where he was. She gave him the correct address and he relayed it to me. With traffic, we were about half an hour away.

Most people would have laughed it off and apologized to their wife and told her to wait at the bar and get an appetizer if she was hungry. But this was Big-Shot British Director, and he was used to having every whim catered to, and used to everything being proper and correct.

So he had a meltdown. Right in the backseat of the rental SUV. And he focused all his ire and godlike wrath solely at me. Screaming at the top of his lungs, emptying every insult he knew. I'd taken my fair share of abuse in The Business, and I'd seen some bad shit, but I had never experienced anything like this.

I didn't apologize, because it wasn't my fault that the production coordinator had fucked me with directions to the wrong restaurant. But I wasn't sure what to do. I just wanted this asshole to stop screaming.

That's when I remembered the break-glass-in-case-of-meltdown advice.

So I fucking floored it.

I ran stop signs, I blew red lights, I weaved through traffic, I slammed the brakes, and a couple times I almost lost it around corners. It was epic—an epic response to his epic meltdown.

At first he shouted at me to slow down. Then he shouted for me to stop.

Fuck him, I thought. I kept going.

And I kept my mouth shut. Just as I had been advised. I didn't say a word.

Then a curious thing happened. In a quiet, almost humble voice, Big-Shot asked me to slow down.

I kept tearing through the streets. Sorry bro.

Barreling around another corner, I glanced in the rearview and saw his face. He was scared. Frozen with fear. Was he remembering that he was mortal? Was he thinking about what was really important in life, and what he would miss when he was dead, and was there really a God, and what happens after you die?

I'll never know. I never asked him. I just kept driving. Driving like I was going to win Le Mans.

After this there was just silence. No words were spoken.

At the restaurant, I came to a screeching halt at the valet, stopping short to really throw him. As he got out of the car, he looked pale and shaken—like he was about to puke. There were no thank-yous or goodbyes.

I peeled away, squealing the tires—just like I was told.

The production team heard about what happened. Since it was the last day of the shoot, there was no talk of firing me. Instead they laughed and quietly told me I did the right thing. That was the last time I saw Big-Shot British Director. He went back to the UK and our paths never crossed again.

But I'm not proud of what I did. This was a fuckup. This was me cracking.

There had been too much stress. Too much abuse. Too much yelling and unfair blame. In the past my rage had bubbled up every now and then, but I had always been careful to keep it down. But not that day.

It erupted in that SUV. I wanted to kill the bastard, and I didn't care if I killed myself in the process. It was true murderous rage—but unlike Method Guy in the murder scene, this wasn't a place where I was comfortable.

∎∎∎∎

Fast-forward ten years. I was a producer now, and the roles were reversed. PAs would chauffeur me around and I was the potential monster. They would pick me up at LAX and I would see the tension in their faces. They were leery of a blowup. Afraid of an epic meltdown.

I would try to reassure them. Exchange a few friendly words to let them know I was no monster. That back in the day, I'd had their job and knew how it felt. And then I would spend the rest of the drive on my phone, listening to messages and returning calls.

Eventually, and without incident, my PA driver would get me to the production office. I'd say hi to the EPs and then meet with my team.

They'd have questions for me. Mostly if there was anything they could do for me personally. Do you need snacks for your hotel room? Do you need any toiletries? Can we get you a coffee? What would you like for lunch?

My production teams were always fantastic. They knew The Business, knew how things worked, and as such they were always trying to take care of The Boss—namely, me. And I, for my part, always did my best to take care of them.

But as The Boss, the constant catering started to bother me. Because once you get comfortable as The Boss, any little thing that makes you uncomfortable can lead to cracking. All that shit you've been keeping down rushes to the surface and you explode.

That's probably what happened to Big-Shot British Director. He'd been ready to crack for a long time—maybe years. Then I took him to the wrong restaurant, and he blew. And now I was afraid, terrified, that I might end up becoming just like him.

My production teams weren't the only ones constantly trying to make me comfortable. It was the crew, the vendors, and everyone else in the ecosystem.

Part of my job was attending casting sessions. This was especially so for commercial projects, where the gigs were shorter and we'd be casting for a new show almost every month. The people at the casting facilities always treated me like a valued client—which made sense since I was the person who hired them. After arriving at the facility, I would park in the VIP lot, and an attractive assistant would take me to the studio where I would be seated on a comfy sofa, given the wifi password, and asked if I wanted anything to drink.

Being a jokester, I'd always ask for Faygo.

In case you don't know, Faygo is a generic brand of soda pop. It's distributed in the Midwest and impossible to find west of the Rockies. It's also the favorite beverage of the hardcore hip-hop group Insane Clown Posse, and so it amused me to ask for it at an LA casting studio as if I were a white-trash Juggalo (whoop whoop!).

Sometimes the casting assistants would politely inform me that they didn't have Faygo, at which point I would ask for a Diet Coke. But sometimes they'd start freaking the fuck out. Because this producer wanted something they didn't have. With panic in their eyes they'd profusely apologize and nervously assure me they would send someone out right away for my Faygo.

At that point (the point of panicked eyes) I'd tell them not to worry about it because I was just joking, you can't get Faygo in LA anyway, and also it's nasty and no one should ever drink Faygo under any circumstances, after which we'd all have a good laugh (even though I was the only one who thought it was funny).

But one day I was working with a new casting director, and we met at a casting facility I had never been to. We sat down, and as usual the assistants asked us what we wanted to drink. I pulled my standard hack joke and asked for a Faygo.

Thirty seconds later the casting director himself came back with a can of ice-cold grape Faygo and asked if I'd like a glass to go with it.

I was stunned. I don't think I'd ever actually seen a can of Faygo in real life before.

I asked, "Where'd you get this?"

He said, "I got it from the fridge." His delivery was deadpan.

I told him I was joking about the Faygo and that I always joke about the Faygo and this was the first time someone actually got me a Faygo.

He shrugged and said, "Well, now you've got your Faygo."

And that was that. I had my Faygo.

We ended up having a great casting session. But I never found out how that can of Faygo ended up in an LA casting studio.

Had he heard about my Faygo joke in advance and sent his assistants to scour the Greater Los Angeles area in search of a generic Midwestern soda just to make sure my absurd request would be fulfilled?

To this day I have no idea.

Ⅲ

At the end of that same session, as I was leaving the studio, I ran into a hot young actress in the elevator. This wasn't the first time. In fact, this was something that happened almost every time. If you want to meet hot actresses, casting studios are the place to be. It's where they gather.

The girl clocked me as someone special. Probably thought I was a director. Since moving to the mountains I'd given up on LA fashion trends. I bought my clothes at the hardware store. I looked like I didn't give a fuck. This had the effect of making me look "creative"—like a director.

She got flirty and giggly. The thing that gets me every time is when they giggle and touch my shoulder. She did the giggle-touch and I felt blood rush to my dick. Thankfully my hard-on was contained by my stiff Carhartts.

By the time we walked out into the parking garage we knew each other's names and she was asking me if I had plans for that night.

I knew she didn't have plans. Girls like that don't go out. It's true what they say about beautiful girls. Most nights they're just sitting at home alone. They're afraid to go out. Maybe not afraid, but they're uncomfortable.

These women—the most beautiful women in the world who come to LA to make it in The Business—have a complex about their looks. When they walk down the street their beauty draws attention—attention from men and women alike. People stare, and they can feel the stares.

Even though you'd think they would be confident in their beauty and appreciate the attention, they get self-conscious. So they wear big sunglasses, and wear a baseball cap low over their eyes. To avoid eye contact they'll keep their head down and look at their phone. And they'll never wear something revealing. Instead they wear baggy sweats.

They want to hide.

They want to be invisible.

Melania Trump does this. She tries to hide in public.

My mom did this too. It sounds counterintuitive, but life isn't easy for beautiful women. There's a loneliness that comes with that level of beauty.

But in the parking garage of the casting studio, away from prying eyes, this girl was confident.

And she was radiant.

And she was horny. I saw her blush as we chatted. I'm sure my face was flushed too.

This wasn't just an opportunity to bang a hot chick. This was a chance to burn down my life. And it would have been a lot more fun than a plane crash.

But we didn't make plans. I didn't take the bait. And no, I didn't tell her I was married with kids—because that would have made me even more desirable.

Women like that love married guys.

I politely (and truthfully) told her I had a lot of work to do that night, but gee it was nice meeting you and hopefully I'll run into you again. Then I got in the car and departed, blue balls and all.

Tempting. But I wasn't going to burn down my life like that. It was exactly how my dad burned down his life. And it was also how my friends were burning down theirs.

Let me say it again: The Business eats marriages. It's so demanding, and so exhausting, and consumes so much time that it's easy for a couple to drift apart. And since you're never around, because you're either shooting or traveling or shooting AND traveling, it becomes easy to imagine a life with someone else—or no one at all.

That's a tempting fantasy for men—all men, regardless of profession. Relationships are hard. Marriage is hard. Fatherhood is hard. And hot women are still hot, even after you're married.

Movies were the worst—or the best, depending on your perspective. You're usually away from home, usually staying in some nice hotel. You're bored, you don't have a life outside of work in this strange city, and you also happen to be surrounded by a bunch of attractive people in the exact same situation, and so everyone starts fucking.

But it's not just the typical male/female dynamics. There's something else at play. When you get on a movie and immerse yourself in this strange world of life on set, it's like entering a fantasy world—or maybe a bizarro world—where the normal rules don't apply.

Truffaut's Day for Night is the most accurate movie about making movies. Among other things it illustrates the sexual dynamics of working on set. Without revealing any spoilers: everyone is fucking everyone.

So regardless of marital or relationship status, people will hook up for the duration of the film. Some people call it getting a "set spouse" or having a "showmance." And then the movie wraps and you go back to your real spouse like nothing happened. You leave bizarro world and go back to reality.

Needless to say, this type of behavior is not beneficial when trying to hold together a long-term relationship.

When I was single it was fun. But I mostly stopped doing movies when I got married. Aside from money, the hook-up culture was part of the reason. My wife stopped doing movies too—at least out-of-town movies, because out of town is where the drama happens.

And no, we never discussed this. It was an unspoken agreement. We didn't need to talk about it. We both knew what would happen.

But now I was away from home. And lonely. And miserable.

And let me tell you, nothing—absolutely nothing—makes you feel better than a beautiful woman. No watch, no car, no fancy dinner, no drug, no amount of money. Nothing will make you feel as good as you'll feel with a beautiful woman on your arm. It's not about sex—it's about affirmation.

My other producer friends were discovering this. They had the same issues I did. The same stress, the same anxiety. And they found that other women could heal them. At least, temporarily.

It was fine until they got caught.

But then again, they wanted to get caught.

Because you can't blow up your life if you don't get caught.

We were having lunch in Santa Monica.

I was sober at the time. He was drunk. On the verge of tears.

He was slamming beers, but it wasn't helping. I knew that feeling and I suggested we find an AA meeting. But he wasn't ready for that. It has to get pretty bad before you're ready. He still had a ways to go.

I loved this guy. We came up together in The Business. Now we were both producing. We shared the same interests, the same worldview, the same sense of humor. It was a close friendship.

He had met his wife at the beach. As I recall he was day-drinking. She was roller skating with friends.

He had just broken up with his girlfriend and things moved fast. Pretty soon they were living together, then engaged, then married, then she was pregnant.

She came from a stable loving family, was a former sorority girl; now she worked for a big corporation. Her life was predicated on stability, on constancy, on permanence. But now she was married to a guy in The Business. Where nothing is stable and nothing is constant.

She didn't understand the hours. Didn't understand why we had to work so late. When we were on a project we never knew when we were coming home. On a job you don't ask "When are we done?" because there's no answer. We're done when we're done.

My wife, who was also in The Business, knew better than to ask me what time I was coming home. My friend's wife didn't.

The Business is too demanding, too intense. And it's not just a career, it's a lifestyle. When you're on a project you're all in—one hundred percent. You don't have time for anything or anyone else.

Not only are the hours crazy, it's financially unstable. Once the project is over, you're done. You've worked your way out of a job. And there's no income coming in until the next job comes along.

As for the next job, you usually have no idea when or what it might be. And even though you have (potentially) an extended amount of free time between projects, you can't plan a vacation or even a weekend away because a) you don't want to spend the money, and b) you need to be available when the call comes. Because they're not going to wait for you and your "life"—they'll go with someone else before they delay the project.

It's hard to plan for the future when you can't estimate how much money you'll make. This is inconceivable to someone with a steady corporate career. And my friend's wife never understood that.

As his marriage started to fail, he began to act out.

It started with nudes. He was adept at getting women to send them. I know this because he would forward them to me. I had to tell him to stop. Not just stop sending them to me—just stop completely.

But he didn't stop. One day he left his phone on the kitchen counter, and she saw.

I think he wanted her to see the pictures.

You don't get caught unless you want to get caught. It was some sort of weird, passive-aggressive power play. As in, "Look at these photos, bitch. I'm still attractive to other women. This is who you're competing against, so have some respect."

They had a baby at this point. I guess he thought she'd never break up with the father of her baby. But it didn't play like that. She kicked him out. He couched surfed for a bit. Then he promised to stop and she took him back.

But he didn't stop. He started sleeping around for real. He even used me as an alibi. Except he didn't tell me I was the alibi.

Eventually, he got caught. She texted me. Asked me if we were hanging out. I told her I hadn't seen him in weeks. And that was it. He got busted—just like he wanted to get busted.

And now we were having lunch and he was drunk.

He was confused and upset. On the verge of tears. Asking me why does he keep doing this? Why can't he hold it together? Why does he keep sabotaging his relationships?

I had no answers for him. Because I had the same questions. Why did I want to burn down my life? And was I heading for the same end?

The worst part is I felt just like he felt. I knew it deeply and intuitively. But even though I knew this about myself, I didn't have the language to articulate it. I didn't have any way to express it.

If I would have had the language, maybe I would have said something to actually help him. To let him know his situation wasn't unique and he wasn't alone. And I was there to help him. And maybe we could help each other. Because he was a good friend and, again, I loved this guy.

But I didn't have anything to say. Nothing helpful at least. I only had the bog-standard guy advice of "quit drinking and get back in the gym." But that wasn't right. That wasn't the correct thing to say. That wasn't what he needed.

So we finished lunch and I left him alone with his misery. And he left me alone with mine.

His wife ended up taking him back—for a time anyway. Then it started up again. I think she started cheating too. Now they're divorced. It's usually for the best in these situations.

After the divorce, he got out of The Business. He works in marketing now. It's a 9-to-5 job. It's stable.

And I think he's happy.

■■■■

The years went by and I kept commuting. I never fully cracked, I never unfairly lashed out at a PA, and I didn't blow up my marriage with some hot young starlet.

But things changed. The budgets were steadily shrinking. I could no longer afford to hire people to do all the various tasks that needed to be done, so more work was put on my plate.

And more and more I was being asked to work uncompensated hours. In the beginning of my producer run I'd always kick in a few free days of labor. But by the end I was putting in free weeks, and sometimes free months, on every project.

And something else changed too. There was a creeping femininity.

In the world I came up in, there were what I like to call Big Swinging Dicks (BSDs). These were men, but sometimes women, who were IN CHARGE. They were empowered to make deals and decisions to get things done.

Love him or hate him, Donald Trump is a great example of a BSD. He gets things done.

In the movie Pulp Fiction, Winston the Wolf (played by the great Harvey Keitel) is the perfect producer BSD archetype. Attending to a crisis where a dead body needs disposal, he rings the bell, introduces himself, and states "I solve problems." And then in an even, common-sense manner, he proceeds to solve the problem, and calms everyone down in the process.

That's what I did as a producer. I solved problems. I did it calmly and professionally. I did it like a man.

But I found my masculinity was no longer welcome. Women tend to solve problems by freaking the fuck out, and I was expected to do the same. And there were no more individuals

I could cut deals with. Instead there were "teams" comprised of women, gays, and feminized men.

Today, this is how most of corporate America is run. And Hollywood is no different. These whiny emotional feminized types had always been in the background, but tough men—the BSDs— had always been in charge. But that changed with Me Too. The BSDs were forced out and the corporate women took over.

Now, instead of being able to cut a deal over a single phone call, I'd be informed that the person I was talking to needed to "get with the team and circle back." And everything needed to be in writing. I found myself sending out long cover-my-ass-type emails and CCing everyone on "the team."

I would use exclamation marks! to make my emails appear more positive! and feminine! I came up in a world of gruff men and women, but now positivity! was important! So I tried my best! to remain! positive!

I was also spending an inordinate amount of time dealing with contracts. There were no more verbal or handshake deals, because the type of trust that only exists between men was gone. You can only make a handshake deal with an honorable person, and the honor was gone.

And then one day it just stopped. It stopped being fun. The joy was gone. And I was over it.

So, in the summer of 2019, I walked away from producing. I gave it all up: the prestige, the travel, the expensed dinners, the beautiful women, the nice hotels, the occasional corporate jet trip, and the eager young PAs who would drive me around and order me lunch and pick up my laundry.

But I didn't entirely leave The Business. I started doing crew work locally in the mountain state we call home. It was just something to do until "I figured it out," but this new work turned out to be a great gig. In fact, I loved it. I really did. (Honest.) So I joined the union and became a full-fledged crew member.

It's still hard work, and it's still long hours, and it can be absolutely stressful, but I'm responsible for less than I was as a producer. I no longer need to control everything. And I rarely fly anywhere.

And at the end of the day, when the work is done, then I'm done too. I can leave the stress of the day behind and go home to my family. And be a husband. And be a dad.

▰▰▰▰

Before 2019, when I was still traveling and still producing, what I really wanted was to get home. To get out of LA and be stuck at a train-crossing in the middle of the night.

Back to a place where I could downshift and unwind and not be someone important, not be someone that people tripped over themselves to cater to and please, not be someone they were afraid of or trying to suck up to.

I'd get in late from the airport, then I'd sleep late. But not so late that I would miss picking up the kids from school. My favorite part was coming home, and the best part of coming home was seeing the kids again.

I'd drive to the school and get a spot in the pickup loop. I'd look around at the other parents, who were for the most part people I didn't know.

I didn't know them because I was gone so often. I was never at the school events. I didn't take my kids to the endless stream of birthday parties and barbecues where I would be asked, "So what do you do?"

It's hard enough to form new personal relationships as an adult, but it's almost impossible when you're never around.

I'd look at the other parents waiting for their kids and wonder who they were and what they did. And I'd wonder what they thought of me. How much do they know about me?

Do they know what happens when I go out for sushi and let slip that I'm a producer? Have they ever taken a casting-studio elevator ride with a lonely starlet?

Do they know that I've partied with famous actors? And do they know how boring it is?

Have they been inside the kitchen of the French Laundry? Do they know what extreme sleep deprivation feels like? Or what it's like to overhear famous actors doing butt stuff in a Star Waggon?

Have they been close to fame? Do they know how empty it is?

And what about my parents? Do they know who they were, and how I was raised?

Do they know how miserable I am? That every time I get on a plane to LA I imagine myself dying in a fiery crash?

Do they know how ambivalent I am about my life? About how my deep love of home and family clashes with my fantasies about burning it all down and running away to a place where I can't be found?

Do they know there's a crack in my soul that can't be filled and can't be repaired? Not by work, not by love, and certainly not by fame?

But then I realize they're not thinking about me at all. Why would they? They have their own lives, and their own problems, and their own secrets. Like we all do.

I'm just another dad in old jeans and a hoodie with a dirty truck living in a small city in a mountain state picking his kids up from school.

They don't care about me.

They don't even notice me.

I'm anonymous.

I'm invisible.

And that's the way I like it.

About the Author

After being discharged ████████████ due to ████ ████ Rambo Van Halen began ██████████ ████ in the film industry. He's responsible for ████ ████ films including ██████ and █████████ ████████████ He has █████████ celebrities such ████████████ and ████████ Rambo lives in ████ ████████████████ with his ██ and family of ████ ████████████ cheese and ████████████

It ████████ noted ███████████████████████ bad idea ██████ or ██████ Rambo.